W9-AEO-344

A Ragged Mountain Press
WOMAN'S GUIDE

POWERBOATING

A Ragged Mountain Press
WOMAN'S GUIDE

POWERBOATING

SANDY LINDSEY

Series Editor, Molly Mulhern Gross

RAGGED MOUNTAIN PRESS / McGRAW-HILL
Camden, Maine • New York • San Francisco • Washington, D.C. • Auckland
Bogotá • Caracas • Lisbon • London • Madrid • Mexico City • Milan
Montreal • New Delhi • San Juan • Singapore • Sydney • Tokyo • Toronto

Look for these other Ragged Mountain Press Woman's Guides

Backpacking, Adrienne Hall
Canoeing, Laurie Gullion
Climbing, Shelley Presson
Fly-Fishing, Dana Rikimaru
Golf, Susan Comolli
Mountaineering, Andrea Gabbard

Sailing, Doris Colgate
Scuba Diving, Claire Walter
Sea Kayaking, Shelley Johnson
Skiing, Maggie Loring
Snowboarding, Julia Carlson
Winter Sports, Iseult Devlin

• •

Ragged Mountain Press

A Division of The McGraw·Hill Companies

10 9 8 7 6 5 4 3 2 1
Copyright © 2000 Sandy Lindsey
Foreword © 2000 Molly Mulhern Gross

All rights reserved. The publisher takes no responsibility for the use of any of the materials or methods described in this book, nor for the products thereof. The name "Ragged Mountain Press" and the Ragged Mountain Press logo are trademarks of The McGraw-Hill Companies. Printed in the United States of America.

Library of Congress Cataloging-in-Publication Data

Lindsey, Sandy.
      Powerboating / Sandy Lindsey.
            p.   cm.—(A Ragged Mountain Press woman's guide)
      Includes bibliographical references and index.
      ISBN 0-07-135702-5 (alk. paper)
      1. Motorboats. 2. Boating for women. I. Title.
            II. Series

GV835.L54 2000
797.1'25—dc21   00-033289

Questions regarding the content of this book should be addressed to
Ragged Mountain Press
P.O. Box 220
Camden, ME 04843
http://www.raggedmountainpress.com

Questions regarding the ordering of this book should be addressed to
The McGraw-Hill Companies
Customer Service Department
P.O. Box 547
Blacklick, OH 43004
Retail customers: 1-800-262-4729
Bookstores: 1-800-722-4726

This book is printed on 70# Citation.

Printed by Quebecor Printing Company, Fairfield, PA
Design by Carol Inouye, Inkstone Communications Design
Production management by Janet Robbins
Page layout by Shannon Thomas
Edited by Shana Harrington, Charlie Doane, and D. A. Oliver

Illustrations on pages 48–49, 51, 55, 66, 76, 92, 96, and 100 by Elayne Sears. Illustrations on pages 28–29, 35, 40, 44, 47, 63, 65, 67–68, 77–79, 84, 115, and 117 by Jim Sollers.

Photographs courtesy the author unless otherwise noted: page 36 courtesy A. B. Inflatables; page 102 (top) courtesy ACR Electronics; page 58 (left) courtesy Billy Black/Offshore Sailing School; pages 13, 83 courtesy Christopher Cunningham/Stock Newport; pages 13–14, 16 (bottom), and 123 courtesy Boston Whaler; page 38 courtesy Corbis Images; page 129 (bottom) courtesy Florida Keys TDC; page 124 courtesy Glacier Bay Boat Company; pages 25 and 127 courtesy Honda Marine; pages 20 and 33 courtesy HydraSports; pages 90 and 94 courtesy Jerry Martin Associates; page 17 courtesy Chris Kelly; page 108 courtesy Kwik-Tek; pages 15, 22, 32, 37, 41 (bottom), 52, 69, 81, 84, 89, 103, 118, 121–122, 129 (top), and 130–131 courtesy Bill Lindsey; page 70 courtesy Nitro Marine; page 53 (top) courtesy NOAA; pages 95 and 133 courtesy Photodisc; pages 53 (bottom) and 61 courtesy Raytheon; pages 19, 27, and 112 courtesy David J. Schuler; pages 58 (right) and 73 courtesy Sea Line Company; page 102 (bottom) courtesy Skyblazer; pages 80 (top), 98–99, 126, and 128 courtesy Stearns; page 21 courtesy Velocity Marine; and pages 34 and 93 courtesy Zodiac.

ACR Mini B2, ACR RapidFix, Betadine, *Boating*, Boatwise, Bruce, CQR, Danforth, Delta, Dramamine, Float Coat, Fortress, Halon, Hook & Tackle, Leatherman, Sea Tow, Shoes For Crews, SOG PowerPlier, Spyderco Mariner, Star brite, Sunbrella, TaskMaster, Teflon, Top-Sider, Trek-Kit, United States Power Squadrons, WD-40, and West Marine are registered trademarks.

• •

"I love the feel of the breeze and the
sun when I'm boating. It's a great
blend of excitement and relaxation."

—Paula Greene, Charlotte, North Carolina

• •

Foreword

"Here, you dock her," my brother-in-law said with a grin. We had been out on the wide open river, wind in our hair, sun shining. Back in the middle of the channel I had taken the wheel and driven the boat reluctantly, inching the throttle up ever so slowly, wondering just how far it really needed to go make the boat go too fast. With my brother-in-law's encouragement I had even managed to turn the boat in a full circle, bouncing over our own wake, moving that throttle back to a slower speed to lessen my fears of flipping the boat. Hard to starboard all around, straight, then hard to port all round. The steering began to make sense. The throttle and I had a more difficult time. Pushing it forward seemed to make it go too fast, yet easing on back I'd often bring it too far and wind up in neutral, going nowhere.

Cautious? You bet. My two young children were on board, as were my sister's two little ones. While the day was bright with Maine sunshine and the river wide with opportunity, I knew better. Lobster pots dotted the river, turning what could have been a wonderful, wide learning path into a slalom course. My stint at the helm lasted under 5 minutes, but in those minutes I assessed a few things. I knew I wanted to learn to drive that powerboat, knew that someday I'd be back—I'd be the one launching and driving for the day. But on that first day I discovered that the learning conditions weren't right for me. The little kids worried me: what if I flipped while turning? what if I lurched us ahead too fast and ejected one of them over the side? And what of my husband and my brother-in-law, both there to scrutinize and correct at the first sign of my difficulty?

"No thanks, not today," I replied to my brother-in-law at the offer of docking. I knew better than to try to learn while simultaneously watching my children or in the presence of my spouse. But while I didn't have my first full powerboat lesson that day, I did discover the joy of driving a powerboat, discovered that with the right encouragement I could probably figure out how to fit powerboating into my life. That day on the river convinced me of the need for *Powerboating: A Woman's Guide*. This book covers topics I would have liked to learn that day, in an atmosphere I didn't have: a quiet, focused environment free of distractions. We've done our best to mimic the learning conditions of a woman's instructional clinic in The Ragged Mountain Press Woman's Guides.

What's so different about the way women learn? If you're like me, you want to hear a description of a method or tactic before launching into it. I'm a fan of the talk-it-over-and-think-it-through-first school of learning. I prefer to ask questions *before* I'm asked to take the boat into the dock. And I like to learn in a group so I can hear other folks' questions—and know I'm not the only one wondering how to slow the boat, or speed it up. There's a sense of camaraderie, honesty, and just plain fun. Here you'll find lots of women's voices: your instructor's, of course, but also voices of women from all walks who love the outdoors. *Powerboating: A Woman's Guide* provides solutions, advice, and stories from women who have done what you are about to do: learn to drive, maintain, and enjoy a powerboat.

I hope Sandy's words and approach help get you out exploring and enjoying, by yourself or with a friend. I'll look for you out there.

Between boating trips, drop us a note to tell us how we're doing and how we can improve these guides to best suit you and your learning style.

MOLLY MULHERN GROSS
Series Editor, The Ragged Mountain Press Woman's Guides
Camden, Maine
July 2000

An avid outdoorswoman, Molly Mulhern Gross enjoys running, hiking, camping, sea kayaking, telemark skiing, in-line skating, biking, and snowboarding. She is Director of Editing, Design, and Production at Ragged Mountain Press and International Marine.

CONTENTS

 **CONTENTS**

Acknowledgments

No book is a solo project, and *Powerboating: A Woman's Guide* is no exception. Many of those who helped in the process did so unwittingly many years ago as they encouraged me in developing a love affair with powerboats and the water. These include my family and friends throughout the years, and especially my parents, Martha and Tony, who taught me the best way to learn is to simply get out there and do it; and Terri Mabe, who taught me that a woman can do anything she sets her mind to.

Others who provided more recent assistance include Jeff Tieger of Star brite; Terry Dunagin and Dean Kutie of Boston Whaler; J. J. Marie, Brad Jennings, John Quinn, and Geri Haber of Zodiac; Nick and Mike Miller of Donzi Marine; Bill Pegg of Sunny Isles Marina and Chaparral Boats; Katie Mitchell of Bass Pro Shops and Tracker Boats; Laura Martin; Wanda Kenton-Smith; Jeanne Craig; Pam Ruderman; and the women of *Boating* magazine, Rachel Cohen and Nancy Nisselbaum.

The Ragged Mountain Press editors and designers have my eternal gratitude for all their patience and hard work: Molly Mulhern Gross for creating, developing, and keeping alive the vision of the Women's Guide series and for having confidence in my abilities; Deborah Oliver for once again guiding me along as we create another book we're both proud of; Janet Robbins for her technical advice and vision; Tom McCarthy for the fateful call that started this whole process; and last but not least to Jon Eaton, just because.

And finally to my husband, Bill Lindsey, whose encyclopedic knowledge and love of the sport was invaluable, and who understood all those midnight hours I spent writing this book. Thank you for making me do it right, keeping it clear, and for sharing the vision of introducing powerboating to women everywhere.

Introduction

"The sea is so large yet my boat is so small" is the sobering thought I have nearly every time I pull away from the dock. Whether I'm on the ocean or cruising across a freshwater lake, I never fail to get a rush of excitement tempered by the knowledge that I'm to some degree literally casting myself to the whims of Nature as I venture out on the water where anything can happen despite my best intentions or preparations. No matter if I'm at the helm of my 15-foot Boston Whaler or skippering a 75-foot yacht, the basics are the same, and so is the feeling of unbridled joy at being on the water again. And now that women represent the fastest growing segment of the boat-buying market, this is an exciting time as manufacturers and the boating industry as a whole begins to focus on the needs and desires of women boaters.

Although my early boating kept me close to shore, as I grew so did my sense of adventure, and I started making longer passages over open waters. I had my own small outboard-powered boat before I had a bike, and I spent endless hours exploring the waters around my hometown, learning about how boats worked, how to keep an outboard motor functioning on my limited allowance. I also learned how the wind, water, and I were intertwined, with the actions of one somehow affecting the other. Some lessons I learned from the people I befriended at the local marinas and fuel docks, while some I learned on my own, often the hard way. Nevertheless, time spent on the water equaled adventure and freedom, and it was all worthwhile.

Powerboating: A Woman's Guide teaches the basics of powerboating the way I'd like to have been taught. I often found myself wishing I had an older mentor who could take me gently by the hand and say "here's a better way to do that." Because powerboating is exciting, any knowledge gained spurs the student to want more, so this book is designed to give you as much as you can absorb, but in doses you can easily absorb. No book will be able to tell you everything about boating, simply because once undertaken, this is an avocation that will continue to teach you lessons for as long as you pursue it, and no one has yet "learned all there is to know."

This book will whet your appetite while giving you the knowledge you need to get out on the water and put the theory into practice. Powerboating is truly a learn-as-you-go sport, but I'll teach you the basics you need to gain enough confidence to get out there and learn more. You're about to join a select sorority of women who gave in to the lure of the water—whether your obsession is deep-sea fishing, scuba diving, or even living the dream of moving aboard your own boat, you share with all other female boaters the exhilaration that comes with taking charge of your surroundings every time you pull away from the dock, completely in command of your own small floating space. This book will provide answers to questions like "How do I get started?", "Can I do this by myself?", and my personal favorite, "How do you do this?"

Powerboating: A Woman's Guide was written for you if you've never actually been on a boat, and it was written for you if you have years of experience on the water. Age is no barrier to this sport, and neither is geography—you'll find powerboats in every state, anywhere there's water and the desire to be on it. I explain all the basic concepts of powerboating so you can learn at your own rate, and when you're ready, you'll be set to take your own boat out on your own adventures.

Now let's get started, because the sun is shining, the wind is soft and inviting, the water's calm, and it's time to go boating!

Chapter 1

WOMEN AND POWERBOATING

A 20-foot bowrider is a perfect entry-level powerboat.

It's a bright clear day with a gentle breeze and not a cloud in sight. Behind you is a world full of ringing phones, honking horns, and congested traffic, but on the water in a powerboat, there's only the sound of the water rushing past the hull and an occasional seagull wheeling overhead. Being on a powerboat brings me an unrivaled feeling of freedom, along with a sense of satisfaction that comes from knowing I'm self-reliant when I'm on the water. With one hand on the steering wheel and the other on the throttle, I'm in complete control not only of the boat, but also of all my immediate surroundings—something that cannot be done on land. My boat is like a small, portable island I can go to whenever I need to get back in touch with myself and to really relax. Whether I'm out alone on the boat, or it's full of boisterous friends, the feeling is the same, and this is a major part of my life.

Your powerboat is your passport to adventure.

I've spent time on boats since I was a young child, but as a young adult I became interested in doing other things. However, as I began a writing career, I found myself drawn back into the world of powerboating. I now make my livelihood by writing about powerboats, but spending time on them is still my primary means of relaxation and allows me to continue to explore this world that brings new pleasure and joy every time I pull away from the dock.

The first time I drove a powerboat by myself, I pulled away with the docklines still tied to the dock, I almost ran over a 4-foot buoy, and I got caught in a downpour—and I loved every minute of it because, finally, I was in charge! My technique has improved since that first time, but now when I cast off from the dock I often recall that first time and think how much easier it would have been if I'd had a patient, encouraging instructor to show me the way and smooth out the rough spots. For you, this book will be that instructor, giving you the support and reassurance you need as you master new skills and become involved in an activity that can provide a lifetime of adventure and enjoyment.

A PERFECT FIT FOR WOMEN

Powerboating requires commitment, concentration, an awareness of what is going on around you, and a good sense of finesse—not to mention a sense of humor—which is why women tend to make excellent boaters. Because women are natural communicators and are well suited to working together as a team, we're quick to grasp and excel at boating. Since powerboating does not require anything beyond ordinary strength and agility, and the engine does all the hard physical work, unlike some other sports, it has no gender gap. The biggest hurdles anyone faces in becoming a good powerboater are realizing

> "Driving my boat requires my total attention, but the funny thing is I step off the boat more relaxed than if I'd spent the day at the spa."
>
> —Teddi Gertz, New Haven, Connecticut

when you don't understand something and not being afraid to ask questions. The best power-boaters are the ones who develop a "feel" for the way the boat responds to the controls and the wind and water conditions. As you become more attuned to these relationships, you'll find yourself becoming a more skilled boater.

THE REWARDS OF POWERBOATING

In addition to being a very effective way to escape from the hectic pace of life on dry land, powerboating also offers a way to achieve inner balance and personal growth, all in a healthy environment out in the fresh air. Powerboating represents freedom and adventure, even if you never stray from familiar waters. Many women become addicted to the gentle pace of time spent on the water as well as to the feeling of accomplishment that comes from mastering a new skill. Because a powerboat is very much like a movable island, and because as the operator of the boat you are responsible for the safety and comfort of all aboard, boaters develop a sense of self-

Fishing is just one of the many adventures you can enjoy when you're a powerboater.

reliance, which tends to bring along an enhanced sense of self-worth. Every woman has her own reasons for boating, but they all relate in some way to the quality of life on the water where she is in control.

One common reason for women to take up powerboating is that the men in their lives are involved in it, and the women want to share the adventure of being a powerboater rather than just a passenger. Others see powerboating as an escape from the frustrations of daily life, in which the frustrations are replaced with the solitude that comes from getting away from others. Others see powerboating as a way to explore a new world they never knew existed. Even the largest cities take on an entirely different perspective from the water that would amaze even the longest-term residents. Some women become involved through related activities like diving or fishing and discover it's more than just a means of transportation. A sense of self-control draws others to the sport, especially those in demanding careers where the actions of persons far removed can have an immediate impact. Still others use powerboating as a way to maintain close ties to friends and family by spending quality time together, building a bond that is strengthened as they work together as a team.

Sheila McVie taking a break during a cruise off the coast of Maine.

WOMEN POWERBOATERS AND HOW THEY GOT STARTED

She might not have been born on a boat, but Patty Jackson has spent a large part of her life ever since on or in close proximity to boats. The children of a marina operator, Patty and her brothers grew up with the water as their backyard and the marina their playground, learning how to operate boats the way other kids learn to ride bikes, navigating small skiffs around the city's miles of waterway years before they could legally drive cars.

After completing college, when most of her friends went on to more traditional careers, Patty became involved in the family-owned marina, becoming a driving force to expand and improve it until she eventually assumed responsibility for daily operations. Whenever she finds her day becoming hectic, she'll slip out of the office for a short boat trip up the river. It may only be a 15-minute cruise, but it's enough to remind her what makes her way of life so special.

Sheila McVie came to powerboating as an adult. An accountant who had helped her husband build a successful engineering firm, she needed focus after his death at an early age. As a tribute to her late husband, she decided to learn how to operate the 30-foot powerboat he had bought as a sanctuary from the pressures of work. Ten years later, she has upgraded to a 45-foot boat and spends six months each year exploring the Intracoastal Waterway, the 3,000-mile-long waterway along the Atlantic from New Jersey to Key West and along the Gulf of Mexico from Florida to Texas. "It was his dream to spend summers cruising, so I cruise to all the places we talked of going, which is my way of keeping his spirit alive," Sheila says.

Terry Dunagin managed to turn a lifelong love affair with boats into what she thinks is the best job in the world. In previous jobs, she used to live for weekends spent on her boat, but now as marketing director for Boston Whaler, she spends all her time on and around the boats and the water.

Terry Dunagin at the helm of her Boston Whaler.

Jeanne Craig about to embark on another of her offshore adventures.

• •

"In five minutes I can be in a completely different world. If it wasn't for being able to see the skyline of the city, when I'm out in the bay, it's just like it was five hundred years ago."

—Judy Miller, Islamorada, Florida

• •

"Sometimes I feel like I'm living a dream, being paid to tell people how great it is to become involved in powerboating," admits Terry. "My friends all have gone on to normal careers, and they complain that my job is a year-round vacation since I'm out on the water at least three days each week. It really does involve a lot of hard work, but it's a dream job that I wouldn't trade for anything. Boat manufacturers and boat dealers tend to be perfectionists, but in their own way they're relaxed because they love their work, so they're a fun bunch to work with."

An active member of the small sorority of women who pursue world record gamefish, Jeanne Craig finds boating more than a way to get to where the fish are. As features editor of *Boating* magazine, Jeanne spent several years traveling to get the stories that describe the diverse joys that come from spending time on the water in boats. In addition to working with other writers, Jeanne also wrote many of the features herself, describing everything from how marine electronics are made to what it's like to spend time on the bridge driving a commercial cargo ship.

Now in another position, Jeanne still finds time to pursue record gamefish. "Spending time on powerboats is how I stay connected with my inner self so I can stay focused on what's really important in my life," Jeanne says. "It's been invaluable in my career in the publishing industry. Out on the water, I find a tranquility that's more valuable than all the money in the world."

By now you see that women who powerboat are just like you and me. Spanning all ages and backgrounds, they lead lives ashore, but they all share the exhilaration that comes from time spent on a boat. These are women who have tasted the exhilaration and freedom that comes from being in control of a powerboat. They are self-sufficient, yet they enjoy the company of others who understand and share these feelings. Powerboating is a sport that bonds mothers and daughters as well as grandmothers, sisters, and aunts. It's a sport that can be enjoyed in all seasons at all ages, no matter where in the world women may find themselves.

Women are getting behind the wheels of powerboats in record numbers.

To truly enjoy powerboating, we need to be open to expanding our skills and adding to our knowledge base. With learning comes competence, and with competence comes increased self-awareness, pride, and self-satisfaction. The best way to learn is to spend time on the water, and the best time on the water is spent in the company of like souls. Powerboating is challenging, but it's also intensely rewarding, exciting, and romantic. It's good clean fun in a wholesome atmosphere where there are endless opportunities for adventure. And best of all, once we cast off our lines, we can truly leave our cares ashore.

Chapter 2

GETTING STARTED

Imagine the feel of a fresh breeze in your face, the warmth of the sun on your skin, and the lush sound of water rushing past—that's the feeling of being on a powerboat. At first, it's normal to be apprehensive every time the boat hits a wake or leans into a fast turn, but with time these feelings will become more natural. You won't notice them, or you may even look forward to them.

When you get a turn at the controls, relax. There's no way to completely describe the feeling of being in control of a powerboat, but to say it's exhilarating is an understatement. Keep an eye out for other boating traffic, stay on a steady course, and feel your face break into a grin as big as all outdoors—this is powerboating!

LEARN BEFORE YOU CRUISE

Before you step behind the wheel, even if you're fortunate enough to have friends or associates who are experienced powerboaters, it's a good idea to get a solid foundation in the fundamentals of powerboating by attending a boating safety or U.S. Power Squadrons course (see chapter 11, Resources). You'll find it's easier to learn from trained instructors in the neutral setting of a classroom where there's no pressure to impress or please your friends or family.

These courses are normally held in the evening over the course of eight weeks, and they will teach you the basics you need to be a safe and knowledgeable powerboater. There's no

HOW TO EVALUATE A POWERBOATING CLASS

• • • • • • • • • • • • • • • • • • •

Although powerboating is largely a "learn-as-you-go" activity best mastered by putting theory to practice at the controls of a boat, anyone will benefit from taking a powerboat operations course. The majority of courses available consist of classroom-only sessions and include courses offered by the United States Power Squadrons and the boating safety classes offered by many state and local parks and recreation departments—either is excellent as a foundation in the basics, or as a refresher course. However, there are also a growing number of on-the-water programs that combine classroom sessions with time spent on the water actually driving boats.

When considering a hands-on course, determine how much time is actually spent driving the boats, practicing skills like docking, maneuvering, and mastering the controls. Consider where the training will take place and what type of boats is used. Practice will benefit you, but obviously the more similar the boat and the waters to those

(continued on next page)

Nothing matches the exhilaration you get from driving a small boat fast.

substitute for on-the-water experience, but by attending these classes you'll learn what to expect, how the various parts of a powerboat work, and how to make every cruise a safe and enjoyable one.

Unfortunately, unlike the wide variety of programs that provide instruction to beginning sailors, there are fewer schools that teach the hands-on, on-the-water basics of powerboating (see the resources chapter). The Power Squadrons and local boating safety courses don't normally include on-the-water classes, but they'll teach you all you need to know to be safe when you actually do get on the water. Powerboating is a hands-on sport, and like tennis or snow skiing, after you read or are taught enough to grasp the basic concepts, the only way to really learn is by actually driving a boat.

Although you may have friends who own a powerboat and will let you operate it, I strongly recommend renting a powerboat at first so you can learn the basics without the pressure of having someone you know watch your every move and possibly criticize you unnecessarily. Rental boats are simple to run and have minimal controls and only the basic gauges (such as fuel and water temperature), which are easy to understand.

Even if you've never driven a boat, a few hours on the water will teach you the basics, and every future adventure on the water only adds to your abilities and confidence. Because weekends are the busiest time on the waterways, try to schedule

• •

"I attended a U.S. Power Squadrons course a few years ago when I wanted to learn about boats. I had friends with powerboats, but I didn't want to ask them all the dumb questions I had. The instructor was very patient with all of us. Best of all, most of the people in the class knew as little about powerboats as I did when the class started, and we all learned a lot."

—Barbie Tomlinson, Galveston, Texas

• •

HOW TO EVALUATE A POWERBOATING CLASS

• • • • • • • • • • • • • • •

(continued from previous page) you will be spending time on, the more meaningful the education will be. Finally, consider the credentials of the instructors—a U.S. Coast Guard Captain's license isn't an absolute must, but it implies both a relevant background and mastery of the basics. At the minimum, instructors should have many years of actual experience in order to be able to offer the most relevant information.

your first few rentals during the week so there will be fewer powerboats sharing the water with you, and so the rental company will be able to spend more time with you to help you understand how the boat operates.

WHAT TO EXPECT YOUR FIRST TIME

Before you step from the dock to the deck of the powerboat, stop and look at your shoes. Are you wearing deck shoes, such as Top-Siders, or athletic-type shoes with rubber soles? If so, you're OK, but if you're wearing any other shoes, the first thing you need to do is take them off! The deck of a powerboat may look steady while the boat's tied up at the dock, but once you're out on the water, the deck can be a wet, moving surface, so you'll need as much traction as possible to keep your footing. Your bare feet are actually the best substitute for deck shoes. (Incidentally, hard-soled shoes will also leave hard-to-remove scuff marks on the deck of the boat.)

Speedboats are no longer just toys for men.

The author, dressed appropriately for a day in the bright Florida sun.

Next, let's see how you're dressed. We'll spend some time discussing the proper gear and clothing for powerboating in chapter 6, but here's the short version: the "official unofficial uniform" of powerboaters is anything casual and comfortable, consisting mostly of comfortably loose shorts and T-shirts in warm weather and cotton slacks and windbreakers in cooler months.

If you've come straight to the water from the office wearing a dress or a suit, you may be more comfortable changing into shorts before you leave the dock. On bright days, sunblock and good sunglasses are a must, and a hat is also a good idea. The sunlight reflecting off the water can damage your eyes; I wear sunglasses with UV-blocking lenses to protect my eyes on even the cloudiest days. The dangers of overexposure to sun dictate that I always wear a hat to shade my face and ears so they don't get sunburned.

STEPPING ABOARD

As you step aboard, keep one hand on the dock and the other on the powerboat. If the boat has a *boarding ladder* leading down from the dock to the boat deck, use it. If there's no boarding ladder and you're uncomfortable stepping off the dock onto the deck of the boat, sit on the dock and scoot forward until your feet are firmly on the deck or sides of the boat and you can step aboard. If the side of the boat is higher than the dock, you'll need to step up onto the deck and then down into the boat.

• •

"I had just moved to Miami, and new friends had invited me out on their powerboat. Nobody had told me what to expect or to wear, so I showed up in 90-degree weather wearing a blue blazer, linen shorts, and what I thought were boating shoes. Luckily my new friends had spare shorts, a T-shirt, and boat shoes in my size, so the day wasn't a disaster. Now it's T-shirts, baseball caps, canvas shorts, and Top-Siders for me."

—Sarah Bass, Miami, Florida

• •

As you step onto the deck, you'll feel the boat move slightly. There will usually be some slack in the docklines, and the boat may move away from the dock as you step aboard, but this is not a problem as long as you don't end up trapped with one foot on the dock and the other on the boat. If you feel the boat is not close enough to the dock, use the dockline to pull it toward you—you'll be surprised how easy it is to move even a large boat closer to the dock. Be sure to step aboard quickly before the boat floats back away from the dock. It's a good idea to have a firm handhold on the side of the boat or on the aluminum or stainless steel *handrails* or *railing* along the sides of the boat.

> "**I** thought the boat was floating away as I stepped aboard! It had just been waked by a passing boat and was bouncing all over, even though it was tied to the dock. Because I wasn't prepared for it and I was trying to look graceful, I fell and cut my knees on the nonskid deck. Now I know to look for and use a handhold as I get onto and off any powerboat."
>
> —Jessie Humphries, Las Vegas, Nevada

The boat is tied to the dock with two *lines* (ropes), one at the front, or *bow*, and another at the rear, or *stern*; these lines are connected to the dock, holding the boat securely in place (see drawing on page 40 and photo on page 51). The lines are tied using simple knots I describe how to make in chapter 4.

Find a comfortable seat where you can see clearly in all directions, and then relax and savor the sensations of being on the water. Soon, you'll have the wind in your face and the warm sunshine easing away any tensions until you're completely relaxed and at ease—yet excited at the same time. You'll quickly see why so many women love powerboating!

NORMAL APPREHENSIONS

Even old salts had their first time on a boat, and it's normal to have questions and concerns, especially when you consider that operating a powerboat has its own set of unique sensations and is unlike anything else you've experienced. Let's look at some of the more common questions and concerns and see whether I can ease your mind about becoming a powerboater.

Do I need a license to drive a powerboat?

No states currently require a license to operate a powerboat; in most states, as long as you're at least 16, you can legally drive a powerboat. Although the only license required is for the boat's trailer, it's still a good idea to attend either a boating safety course or one offered by the U.S. Power Squadrons that I mentioned earlier in this chapter. Even if most of your time on powerboats is only as a passenger at first, you'll gain a lot of confidence and knowledge by attending these courses, and you'll be prepared in case you ever need to help out on board someone else's boat.

A **PFD** is a necessary safety item for everyone on board.

I'm not a good swimmer.

The only thing swimming and powerboating have in common is that they both require water. Lots of women who enjoy power-boating can't swim. This is OK, because with reasonable care, falling out of even the smallest powerboat is unlikely. Even if they're Olympic-caliber swimmers, however, all the passengers on my boat put on *PFDs* (personal flotation devices) before we leave the dock. I'll discuss safety gear in more detail in chapter 8, but suffice it to say that wearing a PFD anytime you're on a powerboat is an excellent idea since a PFD can keep even a nonswimmer safely bobbing on the surface.

I get nervous when the boat rocks. How can I be comfortable on a powerboat?

Because the boat is in the water, there will always be some motion on a powerboat. But the good news is that there's a lot less motion when the boat is actually under way than while it's tied to the dock. As a rule of thumb, the longer and wider the boat, the less motion it will have. Some designs—such as *catamarans*, which have two hulls—are very stable under almost any conditions. (Chapter 3 explains the various types of boats.)

Am I strong enough to operate a boat?

The great thing about powerboats is that they do most of the work for you. Once she understands how a powerboat moves through the water and she learns how to operate the controls of the boat, even a 90-pound woman can safely and easily drive a 100-foot yacht.

How can I control a powerboat if it doesn't have brakes?

This is a question asked by virtually every beginner the first time she looks at the controls of a powerboat. Because the throttle can be shifted to reverse, with practice you can learn to slow or even completely stop the boat. I will go over the proper techniques in chapter 3.

I'm too old/too young.

If you're in reasonably good health, there's no such thing as being too old or too young to enjoy powerboating. There are countless young and older women operating their own powerboats and enjoying the sport. All it takes is a solid foundation in what makes a powerboat move through the water, a good feel for the controls, attention to your boat and surroundings, and the urge to spend time out on the water. If you have any doubts, ask your doctor, but barring any special medical conditions or vision problems that corrective lenses can't fix, there are few reasons any woman can't become an accomplished powerboater. See chapter 8 on comfort and safety for more information about the physical requirements of powerboating.

I get carsick. Won't I feel worse on a boat?

Probably not. Being out in the fresh air on the deck of a powerboat can overcome the tendency to be affected by motion sickness. And better yet, the person least likely to get seasick is the person driving the boat, because she is busy concentrating on the controls, looking out for other boaters, and generally enjoying the experience of being on the water. (I discuss remedies for seasickness in chapter 8).

At age 98, Elsie Thomas is proof that boating is a sport for a lifetime.

What if somebody falls out of the boat?

Unless the powerboat is being operated recklessly or a passenger leans too far over the side of the boat, it's unlikely anyone will fall into the water. But this could happen, so it's important that everyone on board wear PFDs and understand what they need to do in order to help in case someone does fall over. (See chapter 8 for how to both prevent and react to a person falling overboard.)

Is it safe to go out on a powerboat?

Riding on a powerboat is probably safer than driving a car in most shopping-center parking lots. As long as you operate the boat in a careful manner, keep it equipped with all the U.S. Coast Guard–required safety gear (fully described in chapter 8), pay attention to other traffic on the water, and keep an eye on the weather, you'll spend many safe and enjoyable hours on the water. Of course, this doesn't mean you should ever leave the dock without a good first-aid kit on board, since accidents can happen anywhere at any time.

Aren't powerboats expensive to own?

Powerboats come in all shapes, sizes, and colors, and there's one for every budget, whether you choose to buy a new or a used boat. But not all powerboaters own a boat, choosing instead to either rent a powerboat for the day or join a powerboat club. These powerboaters still have all the benefits of boat ownership but not the expense and effort involved in owning, insuring, and maintaining a powerboat.

Because most people hardly ever end up using their powerboats as much as they had planned when they bought them, renting a boat or belonging to a powerboat club is a good option, especially for those women new to the sport who aren't exactly sure what type and size boat is right for them. This technique of "try before you buy" can help you avoid an expensive mistake, and even if you do boat a lot, it may end up being less expensive overall than owning your own boat. (See chapter 10 and chapter 11, Resources, for information on shared-ownership boat clubs and other ways to get involved in powerboating.)

How do I get the boat on and off the trailer?

There's no doubt trailering your powerboat is a skill that requires time and practice to master. The good news is that there are just two primary techniques to learn: maneuvering the boat while it's on the trailer and learning how it feels to actually tow the trailered powerboat on the road. Even if yours is a large boat, you and a friend will be able to load and unload it easily. In chapter 7, I discuss how a trailer works and how to use one to transport and launch your powerboat.

How will I know which way to go on the water?

Many women new to powerboating think there aren't any "road signs" on the waterways, but in fact there are. Most main waterways, rivers, and lakes actually have a system of road signs that tell you where you are and which way to go. By learning how to use a *chart*, which is a kind of road map of the water, you can easily find your way. On most waterways, boat traffic is like traffic on the highway in that you tend to stay to the right side. The other boat traffic knows which way to go, so all you need to do is watch out for other traffic and enjoy the cruise. In chapter 5, I discuss navigational markers, charts, and the rules followed by boaters out on the water.

I don't have anyone to go powerboating with.

Attending a boating safety class or a course offered by the local U.S. Power Squadrons is a good way to expand your powerboating knowledge and meet new friends with whom you can share time on the water. Another option is to attend a boating skills course (see the resources chapter).

What if I need to use the rest room? Is there any privacy on a powerboat?

This is a serious issue, because not all powerboats have a rest room, called the *head* on a boat. Unlike traveling in a car, it's more difficult to "pull over at the next gas station" when you're on a powerboat on a large lake or miles offshore. Many female powerboaters solve this problem by using the same techniques they would on a long car trip: use the facilities before leaving the dock, and keep an eye out for rest rooms along the way.

As far as privacy is concerned, even the largest powerboat can seem claustrophobic at times, especially during stormy weather or when there are a lot of people on board. If you're spending an evening or longer aboard, claim a cabin as your own, or find a quiet spot up on deck where you can spend some time alone. I discuss comfort in full detail in chapter 8.

Chapter 3

GETTING COMFORTABLE WITH YOUR BOAT

The best way to get comfortable with powerboats is to spend time on them, learning how they work and what their various parts are called. The terminology can be a bit daunting at first, but it will quickly begin to make sense and you'll find yourself using it in your everyday language. Let's begin by taking a look at the various parts of a powerboat.

THE PARTS OF A POWERBOAT

Powerboating has its own language, but luckily this language is an easy and fun one to learn. You don't always have to use the correct terms, but just knowing what the terms are will help you understand when another powerboater uses them. The best place to start is at the front, or *bow*, of the powerboat. The open working area of the boat is called the *cockpit*, and the top of any covered area is the *deck*. The *waterline* is where the outer sides of the boat actually touch the water's surface. The sides leading up from the waterline are called the *topsides*, and the rail around the top edge of the topsides are called *gunwales* (pronounced *gunnels*). Rigid vertical posts (*stanchions*) and flexible wire (*lifelines*) run along the sides of some boats about 3 feet above the deck; the lifelines are called *railings* when they're made of a rigid material. The back of the boat is the *stern*, and the underside portion of the boat from its very bottom (the *bottom* or *keel*) to the gunwales is the *hull*.

● ●

"**W**hen I started going out on friends' powerboats, I had no idea what they were talking about when they were using terms like *aft* or *galley*. Now it's fun to use the right words, and I find myself using them all the time."

—Tamara Bledsoe, Pensacola, Florida

● ●

Engines are either *outboard* mounted at the back of the boat on the *transom* or *inboard* mounted inside the boat, normally below the deck. They burn either gasoline or diesel fuel. The *propeller*, or *prop*, is connected to the engine and extends under the water's surface and spins to move the boat. If the boat has one engine and propeller, it's referred to as a *single-screw* boat; if it has two, or *twin* engines and propellers, it's called a *twin-screw* boat.

The right side of a boat, from the bow to the stern, is the *starboard* side, which corresponds to the green navigation light mounted at the bow. The left side of the boat is its *port* side. An easy way to remember this term is to recall that

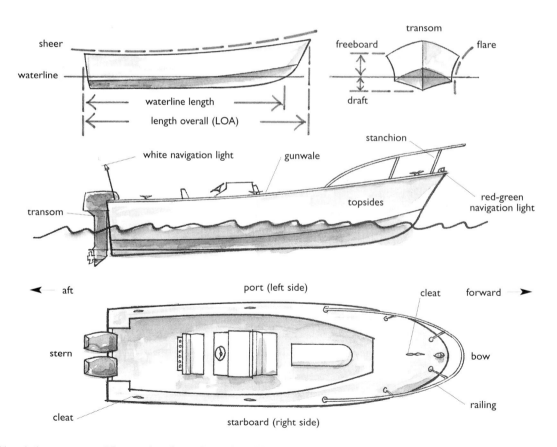

Although there are many different styles of powerboats, they all have a transom, gunwales, a bow, and a stern, and they share such common elements as cleats and navigation lights.

USING AN OUTBOARD ENGINE

Powerboats are powered by either outboard or inboard engines. An outboard engine (almost all are gasoline-fueled) is one that is attached to the transom and hangs outside the boat. Outboard engines are easy to install or remove, and power about three-quarters of all powerboats. Ranging in size from 2 to 300 horsepower, outboards are used to power craft ranging in size from 6 to over 60 feet in length. The benefit of outboard power is increased maneuverability due to the propeller turning in the direction the boat turns, increased room because the engine is located outside the boat, and the ease of replacing an engine. Smaller outboard engines (to 25 horsepower) may be controlled by a tiller with a twist-grip throttle, while larger outboard engines are controlled by means of cables that run from the engine to the helm station.

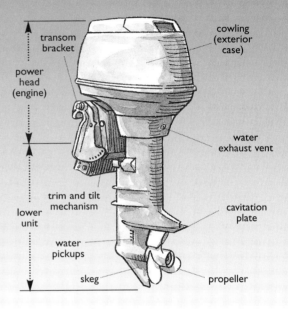

the words *port* and *left* both have four letters, and also that port wine is red, which matches the red navigation light on the bow (see chapter 5 for a full explanation of navigation lights). *Forward* means toward the bow, and *aft* means toward the stern.

The distance from the gunwale to the waterline is known as *freeboard*. The boat's *draft* is the distance from the waterline to the lowest portion of the hull, which is the minimum depth the powerboat needs to operate without running onto the bottom, an action that is called *running aground*. The area under the deck is the *cabin*, and you *go below* (not "downstairs") when you enter the cabin. The opening leading to the cabin is the *companionway*, the rest room is the *head*, the cooking area is the *galley*, and beds are *berths*. There are more terms that we'll go through later, but these are the ones you'll use most often. If you can remember only one thing, make it this: there are no "ropes" on a powerboat, only *lines*!

HOW A POWERBOAT MOVES THROUGH WATER

A powerboat floats because its hull displaces water, which means the hull rests in the water without sinking below the surface. As an additional safety factor, most modern powerboat hulls are filled with flotation materials, such as foam, that prevent them from sinking even if the boat is

"I love the feel of the breeze
and the sun when I'm boating.
It's a great blend of excitement
and relaxation."

—Paula Greene, Charlotte, North Carolina

filled with water (or *swamped*). Depending on the shape of the hull, some powerboats rock more than others as you walk from side to side. Generally speaking, boats with flat bottom surfaces (see the discussion of hull shapes below) rock less than those with round bottom surfaces.

Boats move through the water when the propeller at the stern spins, creating a forward (or reverse) thrust that pushes or pulls the powerboat along. In addition to the force of the motor propelling the powerboat, the wind and water also exert forces that move the boat one way or another to varying degrees, depending on what kind of hull the powerboat has.

Most powerboats have a *planing hull*, made up of flat sections that rise up on top of the water (known as rising *up on plane*) when a certain speed is achieved. The flat planing sections of the hull need not be horizontal, but can run at an angle and may have chines and running strakes to help the boat plane better. A *chine* is an angled corner under the waterline on the sides of the boat, and a *running strake* is a hydrodynamic ridge running along the bottom of the boat.

Rather than a planing hull, large, slow powerboats and most sailboats have a *displacement hull*. These hulls never rise above the water, but always stay well down in the water. They're more fuel-efficient than planing hulls, but they can't go very fast—normally no faster than 10 miles per hour.

Semidisplacment hulls rise partway out of the water and are a popular compromise between planing and displacement hulls.

THE BASICS OF DRIVING A POWERBOAT

Compared to cars, powerboats are simple to operate, especially when you realize there are only two main controls for a powerboat: the throttle and the steering wheel. You'll notice I didn't mention a brake pedal, because there isn't one on a powerboat. At first this may seem like a problem, but honestly, it's OK! I'll discuss how to use the controls in greater detail in chapter 4, but for now, here is an overview of how to drive a powerboat.

The *steering wheel* works the same as it does in a car, pointing the bow in the direction you turn the wheel. The *throttle*—which determines your speed and direction (forward or reverse)—is a little more complicated. Most throttles are levers you push or pull and are set up for right-handed users. These days, most boats have their gear shift and throttle controls united in a single lever. When the lever is centered, the engine is in neutral; push it forward

"I love how I'm part of the
water when I'm out on my
powerboat. I can actually feel
the water as I go through it,
kind of like how you can feel
the road in a sports car."

—Judy Moore, Seattle, Washington

and the boat moves forward; pull it backward and the boat goes in reverse. The farther you push or pull the lever, the faster the boat goes. Some boats, however, have separate levers for the throttle and gear shift functions.

It isn't unusual for many powerboats to have no *speedometer*, but most have a *tachometer*, a gauge that measures how fast the engine is running in *RPMs* (revolutions per minute). RPMs don't tell you how fast the powerboat is going, but usually you can use the tachometer as a rough indicator of boat speed. Many waterways have speed limits, which is one of the many reasons a *GPS unit* (we'll talk about these in chapter 5) is good to have. These little gadgets can show you not only where you are but also where you've been and how fast you're going.

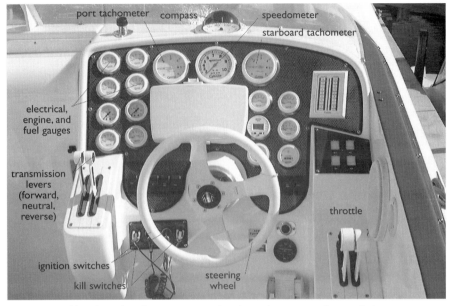

Powerboats with twin engines feature separate throttles, tachometers, and gear selectors so you can easily monitor how the boat is operating.

The engine controls on many powerboats are not very smooth because they're operated by a cable running back to the engine. Don't feel bad if you accidentally shift from forward to reverse; I've done it more times that I care to admit, and so has just about every other powerboater I know. After a little practice, you'll get the feel of your powerboat and will be shifting like an old pro.

TYPES OF POWERBOATS

Powerboats come in all shapes and sizes, from small *dinghies* to huge oceangoing yachts and multiengine racing boats. Boats are measured according to their length from the bow to the stern. This length, measured in feet, is referred to as the *LOA* (length overall). The type of boat you start out on normally comes down to what's available, but even if you have access (continued on page 34)

• •

"**D**riving a powerboat is the most exhilarating feeling I know, and I'm most alive when I'm driving mine."

—Lisa Eustis, Mobile, Alabama

• •

A VARIETY OF SIZES AND MODELS

There is an enormous variety of powerboats to choose from. No matter how you like to spend your time on the water, or how small or large your budget, you're bound to find something that suits you.

Skiffs are typically small (under 18 feet), open boats powered by outboard engines. They're cheap and simple to run and easily launched from trailers. Most often they are used for fishing, or as basic transportation. *Runabouts* are usually slightly larger with comfortable seating for a small number of passengers and a windscreen for minimal protection from spray and waves. They usually have powerful outboard or inboard/outboard stern-drive engines and are used for just what their name suggests—running about at high speed. A very popular form of the runabout is the *bowrider*, which has a step-through windscreen and an extra seating area in the bow.

The most popular sort of recreational powerboat is the *center-console boat*. These boats have control stations in the center of a large, open cockpit area. They range in size from 16 to 25 feet, are usually outboard-powered, and are used almost exclusively for fishing. They have high *freeboard*, or distance from the waterline to the gunwales, and are more suitable for open-water boating than skiffs or runabouts.

Cuddy cabin boats are usually from 20 to 28 feet in length and are the smallest boats to offer full shelter from the elements. A small cabin just forward of the central control station, where you can lie down, use a toilet in private, or perhaps even brew some coffee or cook a simple meal, adds a new dimension to boating. In "walkaround" versions of these boats, the cabin does not extend all the way to the sides of the boat, and, as in a center console boat, it is still possible to move all around the boat without leaving the cockpit. Cuddy cabin boats are normally powered with outboard or stern-drive engines and are suitable for a variety of uses, from fishing to short overnight cruises.

Express cruisers vary in size all the way from 28 to 50 feet, though most are between 30 and 40 feet. They're almost always powered by inboard engines. The idea behind the design is to have a slightly raised control station, or *bridge*, with an open cockpit behind it and a long raised deck forward with enough space underneath for a substantial cabin. As their name implies, these are good cruising boats, comfortable for a week or two of living aboard, with perhaps a little fishing thrown in. One type of express cruiser that has become very popular in recent years is the *picnic*

With an **express cruiser**, you can bring all the comforts of home with you on every cruise.

boat, which has very traditional looks and a large cockpit for entertaining friends.

Flybridge or *sedan cruisers* have larger cabins inside a substantial *superstructure*, or *cabin-house*, that allows for a full *saloon*, or living room, with standing headroom. They are called *flybridge cruisers* because the control station is on top of the cabin. They also have small cockpits in the back, which serve as a back porch, or can be used for fishing. These boats range in size from 32 to 60 feet and have inboard power.

A variation of the flybridge cruiser is the *sportfisherman*, also known as a *convertible*. They also have large cabins

A **center-console design** offers additional cockpit space, making this type of boat ideal for fishing and diving.

with flybridges on top and hence are suitable for cruising, but their cockpits are a bit larger and are equipped for serious game fishing, often with fighting chairs and huge outriggers. They almost always have tall towers erected over the cabin with an extra control station on top. These boats are often very powerful, with inboard engines large enough to run 100 miles or more offshore at high speed in search of large billfish like marlin.

Another sort of cruiser is the *cabin cruiser*, which has no cockpit at all and a cabinhouse that runs all the way to the back of the boat. This design maximizes interior living space and hence is favored

by those who have no interest in fishing and want to spend extended periods of time aboard their boat.

These are only the more basic types of power-boats available today. Other types you may see out there include *bassboats*, which are specialized skiffs for freshwater fishing; *houseboats*, which are almost all cabinhouse; *jet boats*, which are tiny runabouts powered by jet-drive engines; *pontoon boats*, which consist merely of a large, flat deck bolted to a pair of floating metal tubes; not to mention *lobster*, *trawler*, and *tug-boat yachts*, all of which are traditional work boat designs modified for recreational use. Quite literally, the list is almost endless!

SAFETY NOTE

Whenever there is anyone in the water near the boat—such as when your passengers are swimming or if someone falls over and you're bringing them back into the boat—*always* turn the engine off to prevent any accidental injuries. A spinning propeller can do major damage to a human body in no time at all, so don't take the chance of having the engine accidentally slip from neutral into gear when there is a person in the water nearby.

"**A**t first, I was very confused by all the different kinds of boats on the water. To me, they all looked alike! But after I had been going powerboating for a few weeks, I learned to tell the difference between them. It's actually a lot easier than telling cars apart."

—Laura Boyt, Mannassas, Virginia

Always turn the engine off when your passengers are in the water.

(continued from page 31) to a larger boat, I recommend starting with a smaller boat that requires less expertise and is more forgiving. Smaller boats usually have outboard or inboard/outboard stern-drive engines. Neither system is any better or worse than the other, and the choice is simply a matter of preference. All powerboats use the same controls, but learning on smaller boats is easier because you can better develop a feel for how the boat handles.

As you look at assorted models of powerboats, you'll notice their hulls don't all look alike. Most powerboats have one hull and are called *monohulls*. We talk about displacement, planing, or semidisplacement hulls, but hulls also differ in shape. Monohulls can be *flat-bottomed*, which are good for shallow waters but can give a very rough and wet ride in choppy water at high speeds. A *round-bottomed* hull gives a smooth ride but can make the boat tend to *roll*, which is side-to-side movement. Most powerboats have a V-shaped bottom and thus are called *V-hulls*. A *deep-V* hull works best in rough or deep water and is stable at high speeds, whereas a *modified-V* hull is an all-purpose hull found on many recreational powerboats because it provides a smooth, stable ride in all but very rough waters. The *cathedral* hull has three Vs, making for an extremely stable but

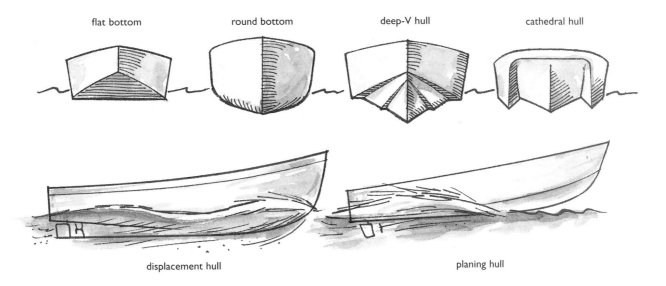

flat bottom   round bottom   deep-V hull   cathedral hull

displacement hull   planing hull

Powerboats have either **displacement** or **planing** hulls. The four main hull shapes can vary in actual boat designs.

sometimes hard and pounding ride. These were made famous by the 13-foot Boston Whaler model.

Although nearly all powerboats are monohulls, a growing trend among manufacturers is the production of *catamaran* powerboats, which have two hulls connected by a raised deck. The advantages of a catamaran design are greater stability, a smoother ride even in choppy water, and faster speeds with smaller engines, with better fuel economy. A *tri-hull* design combines a modified-V with a catamaran design and provides outstanding stability. Some disadvantages of catamarans are that they are more expensive to make and are more sensitive to side winds.

Inflatable boats have hulls constructed of fabric (Hypalon or PVC—polyvinyl chloride) and use air-filled chambers to provide their shape, structure, and flotation.

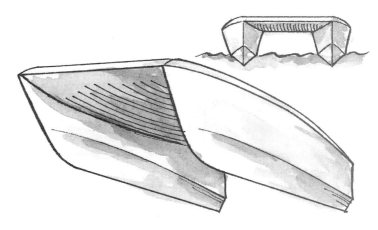

The twin-hull design of the **catamaran** lends it greater stability than a monohull.

A quality **inflatable boat** will provide a lifetime of boating enjoyment yet is easy for beginners to operate.

The class includes *rigid-bottom inflatable boats*, known as *RIBs*, which have one-piece fiberglass bottoms for exceptional maneuverability and increased durability. Found in the fleets of research scientists, various industries, and virtually every nation's navy, inflatable boats can be used by inexperienced operators and offer extreme stability and safety. In addition, they are seaworthy, durable, yet affordable vessels that can be stored in a closet and transported in the trunk of a compact car, making them ideal for city-dwellers or those unwilling or unable to transport and store a traditional boat. Ranging in size from 7 to over 30 feet, inflatables are viable boats no matter where they are found, and their ease of packing and transporting make them perhaps the one boat that can truly go anywhere.

Which type of powerboat is right for you? For now, don't worry about that. First, you need to get comfortable with the different types of powerboats out on the water. How you use the boat will play a large role in determining the type and size you will eventually choose. Once you know how you plan to spend your time on the water, whether taking friends and family scuba diving or waterskiing, you can narrow the search by focusing on powerboats that are best suited for that activity. Small boats tend to be used mostly during daylight hours for short fishing or cruising trips on lakes or along the coast, whereas medium and large boats can be used for overnight or longer trips.

The best way to see a broad assortment of powerboats is to attend a boat show. Boat shows offer a wide variety of types and sizes, all displayed for you to take a close look. You can do a lot of learning just by climbing aboard different boats to see how they are laid out and how it feels to be on them. And because most boat shows are held at exhibition halls or in large parking lots, the boats are mounted on dry land, so you won't be distracted by any rocking motion. As you look at the various models, pay attention to how they

"I had no idea what to expect the first time I went to a boat show. As I walked into the convention hall, I was amazed at all the different sizes, models, and kinds of boats on display. I learned more in an afternoon of walking around than I had in six months of visiting boat sales centers."

—Muffy Burlingham, Freeport, New York

differ because this will help you later if you plan on buying your own powerboat.

No matter what type or size of powerboats you encounter, the basics of operating a powerboat are the same for a 120-foot ship as they are for a 12-foot skiff, although you'll do a lot less damage if you bounce off the dock with the skiff! Larger boats can be intimidating to operate, but with time and practice you can learn how to operate even the largest powerboat comfortably.

A local marina is a good place to get familiar with the various types of powerboats, and find the kind that's right for you.

Chapter 4

LEAVING THE DOCK AND RETURNING

ANTICIPATING YOUR FIRST POWERBOAT CRUISE

It's a gloriously sunny day, and the moment you've been waiting for is finally here. Even if you don't yet have a powerboat, in this section I'm giving you a boat of your own to run. Your powerboat is tied to the dock, with all the U.S. Coast Guard–required gear on board, friends and family safely seated and expectantly waiting, and you're ready to go. In moments you'll be under way, using the knowledge you gained in your boating safety course as you steer out of the marina into the main waterway and start enjoying the sights, sounds, and feelings that come from spending time on the water in a powerboat.

Your boating safety course covered a wide range of material, and you may wonder how you'll ever remember it all. But every time you're out on the water, it'll all come back to you. From the moment you pull away from the dock to the time you return to it, every minute will be full of new feelings, experiences, and lessons learned. It can be overwhelming at first, and that's OK—you've got a lifetime to learn, and the good news is that you'll keep adding to your skills and you'll never stop learning. So you'll know what to expect, let's go through what happens from the time you arrive at the marina to the time you're ready to cast off the lines and pull away from the dock.

PREPARING THE BOAT FOR DEPARTURE

Preparing a powerboat for a cruise is not all that different from preparing a car for a drive. Many powerboats are stored in the water at marinas, so we're assuming here that your boat is already in the water and tied to the dock. Other boaters store and transport their boats on trailers, and in chapter 7 I cover trailering powerboats, including how to launch and retrieve them.

When idle, many powerboats are stored with various canvas or vinyl covers in place to keep different parts of the boat clean. The first thing you'll need to do is remove any covers and then open the cabin and storage compartments to let them air out. On larger boats, cockpit seat cushions are often stored in the cabin. Owners of smaller boats may store these cushions in dockside storage bins called *dock boxes*. Place all the cushions on their seats and secure them in place with the snaps running along their edges. Next, bring aboard any food or gear you've brought along and store it where it won't shift or move while under way.

One of your first and most important safety precautions if you have a boat with an inboard gasoline engine will be to run the *bilge blower fan* before you start the engine. This step is important because gasoline fumes (unlike diesel fumes) are highly explosive and might easily be ignited by a spark if trapped inside your engine compartment and bilges. To avoid this hazard, run the blower fan for at least five minutes, which will disperse the fumes so it's safe to start the engine. This precaution isn't necessary when running outboard engines because they are exposed to the open air, which prevents the buildup of any fumes.

While the blower fan is running, you can check on all your safety gear (see chapter 8 for more information). If you haven't done so already, you should also tune your boat's *VHF* (very high frequency) *radio* to the local NOAA (National Oceanic and Atmospheric Administration) weather channel to find out the day's forecast (see chapter 5 for details about weather forecasts; for VHF-radio details, see pages 95–97). After listening to the forecast, leave the radio tuned to channel 16 so you can hear any weather advisories or distress calls that might come up.

You must also be sure you have enough fuel on board. As a general rule, you should have enough fuel available to use one-third of your supply for the trip out and one-third for the trip back, while keeping one-third in reserve. If you don't have enough fuel, you need to fill your tanks or plan for a fuel stop en route. If you're planning to be out for several hours, you may also want to bring some sunblock, snacks, and drinks. Finally, if you're traveling to new waters, take some time to familiarize yourself with the appropriate chart (see pages 59–61) so you'll know what to expect along the way.

CASTING OFF

OK, the fuel tanks are topped off, plenty of food and drinks are aboard, and the engine is purring contentedly, so let's shove off and get under way. Unlike a car, which is held in place by brakes and gravity, a powerboat at a dock is held in place only by its *docklines*. At first glance, these lines may not seem strong enough to hold a large and heavy boat in place, but they really are. In fact, it doesn't take much to hold the boat next to the dock; if the boat isn't too big and there isn't too much wind or current, you can even do it by gripping the dock with your fingertips.

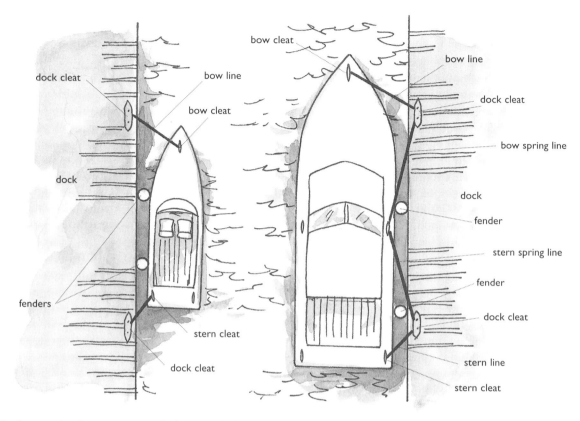

Left: The fastest and easiest way to secure the boat to a dock is with two lines—one from the bow and one from the stern, each leading to a cleat or piling opposite on the dock. **Right:** For larger boats, also use **spring lines**, separate lines that run from a cleat amidships to forward and aft dock cleats and then to the bow and stern cleats to keep the boat better secured. Whenever your boat is docked, you should have **fenders** hanging from lifelines or stanchions to protect the side of the boat from chafing. Adjust the fenders so they hang from the railing against the side of the boat, where they will provide the most protection.

Every boat has at least two docklines (remember, there are no *ropes* on a boat, only *lines*)—one at the bow and another at the stern, each at least as long as the boat itself. Larger boats will also have *spring lines*, which are secured to the middle of the boat and lead to points forward and aft on the dock. Before untying any of these lines, you should try to anticipate what the boat will do once it is free from the dock. Take a moment to watch the water and see which way the current is going; also look at some flags and see which way the wind is going. Is your powerboat being held against the dock by the wind or current? Is it being pushed away from the dock? Is it being pushed up or down the dock?

As a general rule, the first dockline you want to untie and cast off is the one with the least tension on it; the last line to cast off is the one with the most tension on it. This ensures your boat will (more or less) stay in place until you're ready to leave the dock. When casting off a line, untie the end that is secured to the dock and quickly pull all of the line aboard to prevent it from floating under the boat and possibly getting tangled in the propeller.

LEAVING THE DOCK

Once free from the dock, you'll need to maneuver your powerboat by operating its controls. Unless you're running a small outboard with a tiller, you'll be using a steering wheel to steer. Just as with the steering wheel in a car in forward gear, with your hand on the upper half of the steering wheel you turn it to the left to turn your boat left and to the right to turn your boat right. As for the engine, most boats now have a single control lever that combines the functions of both a throttle and a gear shift. To move the boat forward, you simply push the lever forward; the farther forward you push it, the faster you will go. To put the boat in reverse, pull the lever backward. When the lever is centered, the engine is in neutral. To race the engine in neutral, there is a clutch button or switch that disengages the gear shift. Older boats may have two separate engine controls—one lever to shift gears with and another to control the throttle.

Although you're using a steering wheel, you'll find a powerboat handles much differently from a car. A car steers from the front, because the steering wheel turns the front wheels, but a powerboat steers from the back, because the wheel turns the *rudder*, the movable flat piece in the stern that causes the boat to change direc-

Top: Don't forget to retrieve the fenders as you pull away from the dock. **Bottom:** Every time you cast off and motor away from the dock, you're on your way to a new adventure.

tion. This means that when you turn your boat, the stern turns first. The importance of this will be obvious as soon as you try to pull away from the dock. In a car you can pull away from a curb just by turning hard and moving forward, but if you do this in a boat, your stern will smack right into the dock. To avoid this, turn gently away from the dock. You can also give your bow a push off the dock before pulling out so that you don't need to turn so much to get clear.

Of course, another big difference between maneuvering a car and a boat is that a boat is subject to the forces of wind and current. These forces may make it easier or harder for you to get clear of the dock. For example, if the wind is blowing your boat away from the dock, all you need to do to get clear is cast off your lines and wait a moment for the wind to do its work before putting the boat in gear. Or, you can cast off the bow first and let the wind blow it out a bit before casting off the stern. This in effect allows you to turn your boat away from the dock without using your steering wheel and rudder.

When the wind or current is holding your powerboat against the dock, getting clear becomes more complicated. If the wind or current is light, you may be able to get off just by giving the bow a big push and quickly putting the boat in gear, but if the wind or current is strong you may have to *spring* the boat off. To spring out the bow, first run an extra dockline from the stern of the boat to a point well forward on the dock. Then cast off all your other docklines and put your engine in reverse. The thrust of the engine against the dockline will cause the bow of the boat to swing away from the dock. Then you can cast off the line, put the engine in forward, and move away from the dock. When doing this, your stern will swing into the dock as the bow swings out, so you should protect the stern with some extra *fenders*, the soft, sausage-shaped, air-filled objects that hang between the boat and dock to prevent chafing (see drawing on page 40). (Fenders are useful anytime the boat is likely to come into contact with obstacles, either under power or docked.)

As soon as you are clear of the dock, you should ask your passengers to coil neatly and stow all your docklines. Also be sure to retrieve your fenders. You can leave them attached to their lines and lashed in place, but at least pull them inside the boat. One of the most glaring mistakes neophytes make is to leave their fenders hanging over the side for the entire cruise. On a boat, this is like driving down the interstate with your left turn signal on!

GETTING UNDER WAY

Now that you're away from the dock, you can really start learning how your powerboat handles. Steering a boat requires a lot more "feel" than does steering a car because there are more forces involved, particularly the current and wind. Even steering in a straight line may require frequent subtle movements. Probably for the same reason many women are good dancers, so too are we quick to pick up the nuances of steering a boat.

Every boat responds differently to the forces of wind and current, depending on its shape and design, but as a general rule most powerboats react more to the wind. This is because more of the boat

"**G**oing slow should be easy, right? That's what I thought when I was trying to raft up to a group of other boats on the lake. I was coming in nice and steady when the wind suddenly gusted and pushed me right up against another boat, bending my bow rail and making a lot of noise. That taught me to watch how stuff floating in the water is being moved by the wind and currents; it also taught me to use twice as many fenders as I thought I needed!"

—Cathy "Crunch" Carter, Birmingham, Alabama

usually is above the water than below it. The wind also will normally affect the bow more than the stern. This means, for example, when you are running your powerboat at a right angle to the wind, you may need to constantly turn the wheel toward the wind to compensate for your bow's being blown off course. Running into the wind, the boat will steer more easily, because the wind will help blow the bow off to one side or the other as soon as you start turning. Running with the wind, it may be harder to turn, because the wind will tend to blow your bow away from the direction you are turning.

> "**D**riving a powerboat looks easy, and after you learn how the boat works, it is. But it's different from anything else you've ever done, so it takes getting used to."
>
> —Missy Tucker, Port Charlotte, Florida

Current, unlike the wind, normally will affect the stern of your boat more than the bow. This is because most boats have more *draft*, or are deeper, in the stern. Obviously, if you have the wind or current or both behind you, your boat will go faster, and if they are against you, it'll go slower. Also, the slower your speed the more powerful the wind or current will seem. At high speeds, you may not notice them much at all.

To practice driving your boat, find an open area where there's little or no other boat traffic, such as an open area of lake or a long waterway or river. This may seem easier said than done until you realize that even the busiest waterways are normally very quiet during the week. Start by going forward slowly. Push the throttle forward until you are moving forward with enough speed to steer the boat, but not so much that things are happening too quickly for you. Practice going forward, staying in a straight line, until you get the feel of the boat. As you gain confidence, increase your speed. Each cruise will be a little different in terms of wind and current conditions, but the basics will remain the same.

TURNING TO PORT AND STARBOARD

On a boat, as described earlier, right is starboard, and left is port. To turn in either of these directions, you can just turn the wheel right or left. The boat has to be moving in order to turn, and the minimum speed at which a boat will turn is called *steerageway*.

The speed with which you complete a turn is linked to how much you turn the wheel and how fast the boat is moving. The boat will turn if it is moving through the water, even with the engine in neutral, but it will turn much more quickly if the propeller is spinning—and the faster the better. You'll soon find that steering a boat efficiently involves using both the throttle and the steering wheel, and that short bursts on the throttle will help turn the boat in tight places. This is absolutely something you'll want to practice! Take the time to learn how your powerboat responds to the throttle while turning and develop a feel for how much is needed to really kick the stern around.

Although smaller boats (10 to 29 feet) normally have one engine and are turned simply by rotating the steering wheel, it's fairly common for boats 30 feet and longer to be equipped with two engines. On these boats, you can turn by putting one engine in forward and leaving the other

THE FORCES AT WORK

The direction, or *heading*, of the boat is determined by several factors: the force and direction of the wind, the direction and speed of the current, and your particular boat. The factors on your boat that influence heading are the steering wheel, any propeller side force (*prop walk*) on a single-engine boat, and how you use the throttle and engines.

On a single-engine boat, whichever "hand" your propeller has is the direction the stern will tend to move (a right-handed prop, which spins clockwise, will push the stern starboard), which means the bow will move in the opposite direction as the prop.

If your boat has two engines, you'll need to learn how to use to best advantage the maneuvering capabilities of dual engines. The prop on the starboard side is right-handed, and the port prop is left-handed, so forward movement tends to be straighter than on a single-engine boat.

In short, no matter what the boat salesperson tells you, driving a powerboat is *not* just like driving a car, so it will take some time for you to learn the nuances of handling your particular boat in various winds and currents, given your boat's prop and engine.

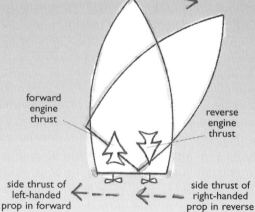

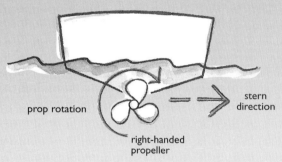

Prop walk with a center right-handed propeller.

You can turn a twin-engine boat on a dime by putting one engine in forward and the other in reverse.

in neutral. Or, if you really want to spin on a dime, you can put one engine in forward and the other in reverse. For example, putting the port engine in forward and the starboard engine in reverse will turn the boat very sharply to starboard. Or, you can turn the boat by putting one engine in reverse and leaving the other in neutral. This enhances your maneuverability in a variety of situations.

Powerboats with outboard or *stern drive* — a type of outboard—engines will also behave differently while turning. Although both of these engine types feature a lower unit that extends out from the transom, the outboard engine is literally bolted to the transom, whereas a stern-drive engine is located inside the boat. These boats don't have rudders; instead, the propeller itself turns when you turn the steering wheel. This allows you to make very sharp, precise turns, even at lower speeds, and greatly increases maneuverability. The drawback is that the propeller must be spinning for the boat to turn, so you can't turn or maneuver with the engine in neutral.

"**T**he biggest thing I had to get used to in driving the boat was the fact there are no brakes! When I got my own boat, I took it to a deserted part of the lake to practice stopping and turning until I was comfortable doing it in front of anyone else."

—Sheila Souser, Kissimmee, Florida

UNDERSTANDING PROP WALK

As you practice turning your boat, especially at low speeds, you may notice there is another mysterious force to contend with. This force is called *stern thrust*, or *prop walk*, and is a slight sideways motion caused by the propeller as it spins in the water. To see how it works, start your boat very slowly while moving straight ahead from a dead stop on a calm day when there is no wind or current. You'll notice that, as you slip the boat into gear, the stern creeps a little bit to one side or the other. On a *right-handed propeller*, a propeller that spins clockwise in forward gear, the stern will "walk" to starboard (and the bow will turn a little to port). With a *left-handed propeller*, or a right-handed propeller turning in reverse, the effect is the opposite.

When turning your boat while moving forward, most of the time you won't be bothered by prop walk. You should notice, however, that your boat will not turn quite as sharply one way as it will the other, because one way the prop walk is working with you and the other it's working against you. Prop walk doesn't happen on boats with two engines, because the two propellers are *counterrotating*, or spinning in opposite directions, and their stern thrusts cancel each other out.

GOING IN REVERSE

Now that you've mastered turning and going forward in a straight line, let's back up—literally. Learning how to use reverse is very important because, as you may have noticed by now, a powerboat doesn't have any brakes! Usually the fastest and easiest way to stop once a boat is moving

DOCKING TO PERFECTION

. . . .

One aspect of boating that can be the most intimidating is approaching the dock. Whether it's a fuel dock, waterfront restaurant, or the dock behind your house, docking can be nerve-wracking because a boat doesn't have brakes and is subject to the effects of the current as well as varying winds. Docking is a skill that requires finesse born of many hours of practice. The only way to learn is by doing, but that doesn't mean you have to practice at the dock—I learned how to dock like a pro by practicing for hours in the middle of the bay, using a nearby buoy as the "virtual dock." I practiced approaching the buoy-dock until I learned to use the current and wind to help me make a smooth approach, as opposed to accidentally slamming into the dock. By maneuvering against the wind and current whenever possible, it's easy to control the speed of the boat, so you can slide right up the dock like an old salt, without any last-minute frantic use of the engine or spinning of the steering wheel. Watch to see how and where the current or wind is trying to push the boat, and use that force to

(continued on next page)

forward is to throw it in reverse. Doing this will make docking easier and will help you keep complete control over your boat.

Unfortunately, backing up isn't quite as easy as moving forward. Just as in a car, you should turn your steering wheel in the direction you want the back of the boat to turn, but the first thing you'll notice is that turning the wheel doesn't work as well going backward as it does going forward. This is because the main thrust from the propeller is now shooting away from the rudder rather than right against it, so the rudder isn't as effective. To get up steerageway and get the rudder working, you'll need to build up a little more speed than is necessary when moving forward.

The other big difference when backing up is that there is much more prop walk. Most boats have right-handed propellers, so usually your stern will try to swing to port as you back up. It will take some practice to overcome this motion, so start out slow and get a feel for how your boat responds. Each boat will back up differently, and at first you may find it a little frustrating. This is when you'll really wish for a boat with twin engines, which is much easier to back up in a straight line.

DOCKING

OK, you've mastered going forward, backing up, and turning. Now what? You want to be able to approach a dock and be in control of your boat the whole time. Too many powerboaters try to coast to the dock, which usually results in their banging into it if they come in too fast. Or, they come in too slowly, end up having the wind or current sweep them away from where they want to go, and are seen frantically clawing at other docked boats as they drift away. How fast is fast enough? I like to suggest you come in at exactly the speed you're willing to hit the dock. This means moving forward at a speed that lets you maintain control of the boat but not so fast as to jar up against the dock. Some boaters prefer to dock by backing into the dock with the bow pointing out and away—this is called docking *stern-to*, and facilitates loading and unloading.

Whenever possible, you want to dock your boat with its bow heading into the wind or current, whichever is stronger, because this will help stop the boat as you approach. You also want to be able to use reverse to help stop the boat, while having the forces of prop walk work to your advantage.

Docking the boat stern-to makes loading and unloading a lot easier and faster.

For example, let's assume you're coming in to a dock in a boat with a right-handed propeller. This means you want to find a spot where you can come in head to wind with the dock on your port side. You tie a set of fenders to the port rail and flip them over the side. You're approaching the dock with your bow pointed into the wind, which allows you (continued on page 50)

(continued from previous page)

DOCKING TO PERFECTION

your benefit instead of trying to overcome it by using more throttle.

And once you've mastered approaching the dock, spend a few minutes beforehand to let your passengers know exactly what you want them to do—to help or stay seated—as you dock. Well-meaning passengers jostling to grab docklines, toss fenders over the side, or snare a piling before you're ready can turn the smoothest approach into a fiasco in no time at all.

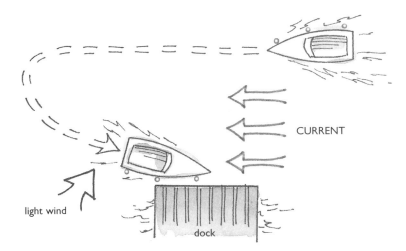

CURRENT

light wind

dock

As you slow to approach a dock or boat ramp, the wind suddenly has more influence over where your boat goes. By determining the direction of the wind and heading into it or against it whenever possible, you can use the wind to make a smooth, safe approach.

NOT A LOT OF KNOTS

Many "old salts" will try to convince you of the need to learn several dozen knots before you can even consider operating a powerboat, but the truth is you only need to know a handful. While sailors need to know many knots in order to secure the variety of sails on their boats, powerboaters can get by with as few as three because we are much less reliant on lines, using them mainly to hold us to the dock, secure anchors, or hold fenders in place. Specifically, the basic knots a powerboater needs to know are the bowline, clove hitch, and half hitch. To tie these knots, though, you need to remember that the outboard end of the line that's fastened to something is called the *working end*; the *standing part* of the line is the part of the line between the working end and the end fastened to the boat, which is called the *bitter end*.

A *bowline* forms a fixed loop at the end of a line and is great when you need to join two lines together. Or, you can make a large loop to slip over a piling when you're docking or to attach just about anything to the end of a line. The big advantage of a bowline is that no matter how tight it becomes, it's always easy to untie. This makes it the best knot to use whenever a line will have a very large load on it, such as when you tow another boat. To tie the bowline, make a small overhand loop on the standing part of the line and pull the working end through the loop (see 1, below). Then draw it around the back of the standing part of the line (2) and back down through the loop, pulling it tight (3). If it helps you remember the sequence, think of the standing part as the tree, the small loop as the hole, and the working end as the rabbit: the rabbit comes up out of the hole, goes around the tree, and then goes back down into the hole.

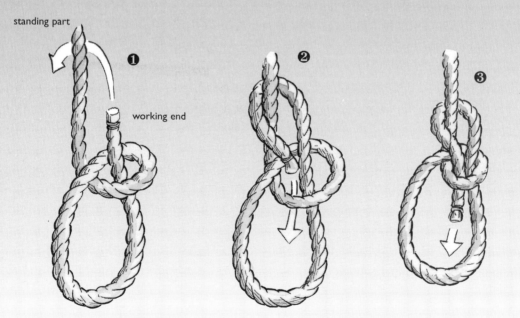

standing part

working end

Bowline.

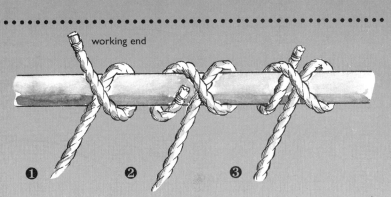

Because the *clove hitch* is held in place by tension, it can be used to suspend fenders from a railing or attach a line to a piling. Run the working end of the line around the object once (see 1, right) and then wrap it around again in the same direction, but this time on the other side of the standing part of the line (2). Finish by drawing the working end between the second loop and the standing part so both ends of the line are pointing in opposite directions (3). Pull tight. To make a clove hitch fast, secure with two half hitches.

The **clove hitch** is a good knot for tying fenders to lifelines and securing a rope around a post.

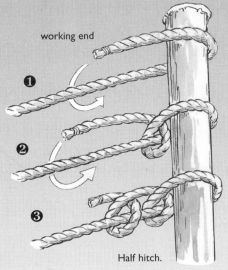

The *half hitch* is a fast and easy all-purpose knot, which is easier to tie than a bowline and can also be used in many situations. You can make a line fast to just about any railing or post by taking a line around it and securing the line with two half hitches. Unlike a bowline, however, a half hitch seizes under load and can be difficult to untie if it becomes very tight. To form a half hitch, loop the working end of the line around the object (1), then pass the working end around the standing part of the line and under itself (2). Pass the working end around and under once more for the second half hitch (3).

Half hitch.

You'll be in good shape if you know only the bowline, clove hitch, and half hitch, but if you go boating in all kinds of weather or anchor in different bottoms, you should also know the *anchor bend*, which is used to tie line to the anchor (see bottom). Draw the working end of the line under the round turn on the anchor ring so it's locked under load. Add two half hitches, and the only thing left is to finish off with a bowline that secures the working end to the standing part.

The knots you don't want to use on a boat are probably the ones you know best: the overhand knot and the granny knot. An overhand knot is difficult to untie once it has been tightened, and you can usually count on a granny knot to slip and come undone at the worst possible time.

If you change your anchors often, you should know how to do an **anchor bend** (right).

> "I learned how to tie knots from looking at how other boaters did theirs. I'm still amazed at how such a simple knot can hold a big boat."
>
> —Betsy Wright, Pompano Beach, Florida

(continued from page 47) to maintain steerageway easily while moving slowly forward. Come into the dock at a slight angle with your bow pointed to where you want it to be tied up. When this point is a foot or so away, stop the boat quickly by putting it into reverse. Your prop walk will pull the stern over to the dock, and there you are!

Another way to use reverse to approach a dock is to line up parallel to where you want to tie off and then quickly shift from reverse to forward and back again, which will make the boat "walk" sideways over to the dock. This isn't an exact science, and the wind and current will have some say in where you go, but once you've mastered it, it's a pretty neat and very useful trick. Like any other maneuver, practice this one before you use it in front of guests or in a crowded area.

FENDING OFF AND MAKING FAST

If your passengers are willing and able, they can help as you leave or approach the dock by being ready to *fend off* such objects as other boats or dock pilings while you maneuver around them. Fending off involves using a boat pole or your hands to guide your boat gently as you slowly move past or around other objects. Be sure you keep your speed to a minimum, and you'll be amazed at how even the most petite female can easily and safely guide a large powerboat past pilings or along a dock. You should never fend off when your boat is traveling fast or put any part of your body directly between your boat and another object, because you may be seriously injured.

You'll also want your passengers to lend a hand getting docklines ashore when landing at a dock. Getting lines ashore quickly and in the right order is particularly important when you are landing in less than ideal conditions. You can use a dockline to help slow and stop the boat if you're landing with the wind or current behind you, or to help hold you in place if the wind or current is forcing your boat away from the dock.

Normally, it is best if the first line ashore is one attached to the middle of your boat. Taking up tension on this line will then pull the middle of your boat toward the dock. If your boat has only bow and stern lines, it is usually best to get the bow line ashore first so that the wind won't blow your bow out of position. You should then quickly make a stern line fast.

Both on your boat and on the dock, you will tie your lines to objects known as *cleats* (see photo next page). Cleats resemble half of a capital I and are firmly bolted to the dock or the boat. The ends of the I, which hold the line in place, are called the *horns*. The cleats on the dock are usually a lot larger than the cleats on the boat, but they work the same way. On the dock, you might also be tying lines around a piling. Whenever you are working with lines when docking, you should first take half a turn around a cleat or piling before pulling on a line to pull your boat into position. This not only makes it easier for you to pull the line but also will keep you from being pulled into the water if there is too much load on the line.

When you are *making fast*, that is, securing your boat to a dock, your bow line should normally lead to a point forward of the boat and your stern line to a point behind the boat. Always make sure the lines lead under your boat's railings—the railing could be bent if a line going over it is suddenly tightened for any reason. If you're tying to a floating dock, your docklines can be short and relatively taut (see photo, right). But if you're tying to a fixed dock in an area with significant tides, be sure to leave your lines a little loose and long enough to allow for changes in the water level.

The relatively short standing part of the **dockline** here indicates the dock is floating or there's no tide. After cleating the line, coil the rest of the line neatly.

KNOTS FOR DOCKING

The good news is that when it comes to tying up your boat, you don't need to know any complicated knots. Here's how you secure a line to a cleat: first wrap the line once around the base of the cleat; then make two figure-eight turns around the opposite horns of the cleat, and finish by slipping a reverse turn (a *half hitch*, see page 49) around one of the horns. This is known as

working end

to boat ....▶

Adjust the length of the standing part of the line before you **tie off to the dock cleat** with one full wrap, two figure eight wraps, and a half hitch. That's all you need to hold virtually any boat secure to the dock under anything less than storm conditions.

BOWLINE VERSUS *BOW LINE*

• • • • • • • • • • • • • • • • • • • •

Your boat's *bow line* (pronounced *bau lĭn*) is the line or rope attached to the bow of the boat. A *bowline* (pronounced *bō lən*), however, is one of the knots boaters find most useful.

A **bowline** tied at the end of a dockline allows you to easily slip the line on or off a piling when docking.

cleating off a line and will securely hold even a large boat in place.

Docklines often have a prespliced loop at one end. If yours don't, you can tie in some loops if you like. When docking, it is easiest just to drop a loop over a cleat on your boat (if the loop is very big, you may want to wrap it twice around the cleat) and then, when you dock, just step ashore with the other end, pull up any slack in the line, and cleat off the free end to a cleat on the dock. Resist the urge to take many wraps when cleating off a line—it won't hold the boat any better, and it will take longer to cast off.

Chapter 5

WEATHER AND NAVIGATION BASICS

WEATHER FORECASTING BASICS

"How's the weather look?" is a question powerboaters are constantly asking one another because we all want to spend time on the water during gloriously clear, calm days without a cloud in the sky. As you spend more time on the water in your powerboat, you'll develop a good sense of what the weather will be like. Developing this sense will take practice observing weather patterns and noting what the various changes signify.

Predicting the weather is too complex to address fully in this book, but we can go over a few basics that will serve you well. No matter how skilled you become at weather forecasting, there will be times when you get caught in the rain or maybe even in a storm. Because it can actually be fun to boat in the rain (it's one of my favorite times because almost everyone else runs for the dock, leaving me all alone on the

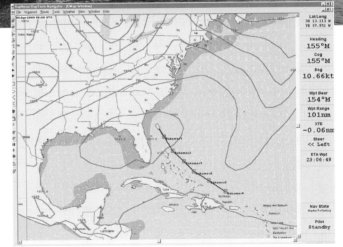

Powerful technology is available to powerboaters to both navigate and keep abreast of weather reports. Here, updated positions of an active hurricane heading for the South Carolina coast are displayed on an **electronic weather chart**.

• •

"To me there are only two kinds of clouds: rain clouds and puffy clouds. And one of the greatest things about having a powerboat is that if I see rain clouds building, all I have to do is drive away from them, over to where the puffy clouds are. If there's nothing but rain clouds in the sky, and they keep getting lower and darker, I head back for the dock."

—Linda Foster, San Diego, California

• •

water) and you don't want to let the weather always determine when and where you go out on the boat, the trick is to be able to accurately predict what the coming changes might be, how soon conditions might change, and when they could be too severe to remain on the water. Unlike folks in sailboats and other nonpowered craft, many powerboaters can simply choose to drive away from or around bad weather, which is always prudent. But it's still important to understand what makes the weather change and to recognize the signs.

Because weather patterns are very different in different parts of the country, specific indicators of changing weather will vary from place to place. As you spend more time on your boat in your local waters, you'll learn what to watch out for. Often, for example, specific changes in wind direction are very reliable omens of changes in the weather. Weather forecasting is as easy as paying attention to what's going on around you as well as listening to the weather channel on your boat's VHF radio and watching the weather portion of the evening news.

In the broadest terms, weather is caused by variations in temperature on the earth's surface that give rise to variations in air pressure in the atmosphere. This is because warm air rises, creating areas of low air pressure, and cold air sinks, creating areas of high air pressure. *High-pressure cells* rotate in a clockwise pattern and create less wind and fair weather, whereas *low-pressure cells* rotate counterclockwise, creating more wind and bad weather. As these systems move, they push along *air masses* of different temperatures; the edges of these masses, called *fronts*, can spread poor weather conditions over a wide area.

Because air pressure plays such an important role in determining the weather, you might want to carry on your boat a *barometer*, a device that measures changes in air pressure. Falling pressure often indicates deteriorating weather, while rising pressure indicates improving weather. The faster the change in pressure, the harder the wind will blow.

TIPS TO AVOID BEING CAUGHT IN A STORM

Sooner or later, you'll get rained on while you are out on your powerboat. If it's just a summer shower, the worst that happens is you get damp and cooled down a bit. A serious storm is another matter, but by monitoring the local NWS frequency (see sidebar page 56 for more information on NWS) and paying attention to incremental or suddenly changing conditions, you won't be caught by surprise. Boating is supposed to be fun, but it is a sport that demands your attention.

WHAT THE CLOUDS MEAN

Clouds are a useful indicator of the weather. Obviously, if there are no clouds in the sky, it's a safe bet it will be a clear day; conversely, if there are lots of low, dark, heavy-looking clouds accompanied by gusty breezes, some bad weather is probably on the way. Clouds form as warm, moisture-laden air rises and cools. As the air cools, it loses its ability to retain moisture. At some point the water vapor becomes liquid, and if the air temperature is sufficiently cold, ice is formed.

Clouds can reveal something about the upcoming or imminent weather if you know how to read them. *Cirrus clouds* are the highest and often develop wispy trailing edges called *mares' tails*—they usually indicate an approaching warm front. Covering a large area of the sky, *cirrostratus clouds* are high, transparent clouds through which the sun is visible, perhaps with a halo; these clouds may signal an approaching storm. *Cirrocumulus clouds* typically resemble large gray and white lumps scattered in the sky, and they signify unsettled weather.

When *cumulus clouds* are white, they're a sign of clear, calm weather, but as they gather and darken, they indicate rain. *Cumulonimbus clouds* are large, dark, and anvil shaped; they will likely bring violent thunderstorms. Low or midlevel clouds, *nimbostratus clouds* are dark and heavy, usually holding steady drenching downpours.

In general, *stratus* clouds are characteristic of stable weather with little wind or moisture. The basic rule of thumb is this: the time it takes clouds to gather, darken, lower, and then form into rain is a

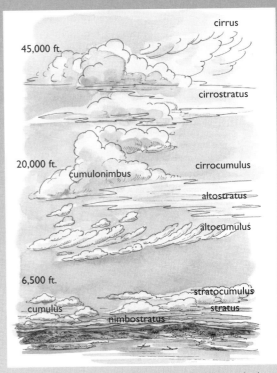

The shape, size, color, and altitude of clouds indicate whether you can expect rain or a perfect day on the water.

good indicator of how long the rain will last. If the clouds come together very quickly out of the blue, the rain will be brief, but if the clouds have been building for hours, you're in for a good soaking. This is generally true of any bad weather. The longer it takes to arrive, the longer it lasts. The quicker it arrives, the sooner it is over.

NWS WEATHER RADIO

The best source of weather information for recreational boaters is the U.S. National Weather Service (NWS), which continuously broadcasts current and anticipated weather conditions over VHF channels. You can monitor NWS broadcasts by means of a VHF radio or a weather radio that is pretuned to the various NWS frequencies.

Weather radios are available in portable versions that can be used at home, in the office, or on your way to the marina. The dial on your VHF radio, whether it is a handheld portable unit or a permanently mounted model, will have a *Wx* (weather frequencies) selector and usually up to 10 dedicated weather channels. Because NWS broadcasts over different frequencies in various parts of the country, try each one to find the strongest signal for your area. By listening to the weather forecasts before you leave the dock, and at least once every hour while you're boating, you'll have an idea of what to expect as the day progresses.

"I'm no weather lady, but after a few years of owning my own powerboat, I find I can tell when it's going to be a good day, and when it's going to rain. I guess you just pay more attention and learn to recognize the signs of a storm coming, like a stronger breeze or dark clouds on the horizon."

—Tamara Eliott, Long Island, New York

Out on open waters in summer months, keep an eye out for *squalls*. These small torrential downpours look like a dark curtain rolling across the horizon and can move at an astonishingly fast rate. Squalls often carry high winds and may pass through in only a few minutes, but because there usually is a line of bad weather behind them, it's a good time to get off the water or out of the area. Because squalls are compact and you can see them coming, it's easy just to get out of their way.

NWS broadcasts emergency storm warnings on local VHF weather channels, and there may even be announcements on channel 16 as well, so you usually have warning of approaching bad weather in plenty of time to get back to the dock or another safe place to ride out the storm (see drawing of VHF radio on page 96). When seeking shelter from an approaching storm, you shouldn't run toward the storm unless you are certain you'll reach your safe haven before the storm arrives. Normally it is best to run in the same direction the storm is moving. If you can't reach a marina or harbor in time, look for a place to anchor or just sit and wait where a body of land can protect you from the force of the wind.

Because storms can blow in faster than you might expect, monitoring a **weather radio** is the best way to know what to expect.

WHAT TO DO IF YOU'RE CAUGHT IN ROUGH WEATHER

Sometimes, in spite of your best efforts at forecasting, you may get caught out in a storm. With proper attention, this won't happen very often, but when it does you don't need to panic. Getting caught in bad weather can be frightening and uncomfortable, but if you act prudently it needn't be too dangerous. Always remember: your boat is much stronger than you are!

If you can't find shelter, the best thing to do is find open water that isn't too shallow. To run away from the land may seem counterintuitive, especially because the waves from high winds may seem bigger in open water. But big waves by themselves aren't a problem; steep breaking waves are the most dangerous, and waves get choppy and break much more easily when the water beneath them is shallow. Most particularly, you want to stay away from what is known as a *lee shore*, a location where you are caught between the land and the direction the wind is coming from.

Steering in big waves is much different from steering on flat water. When the water is calm, you can steer in whatever direction you like, but when a big sea is running you need to adjust your course to the waves. Generally, it is safest to steer toward the waves at an angle of 45 degrees or less; if you must steer away from them, also do so at an angle. Avoid taking the waves directly on your bow or stern and, most importantly, avoid taking them on your *beam*, or on the side of your boat. You will also need to moderate your speed. You want to go fast enough to maintain control but not so fast that the boat is pounding and flying off the waves.

When you anticipate that you will be caught in bad weather, be sure to stow any loose equipment in a secure place before things get rough. You and your passengers should also put on your PFDs, and you should caution your passengers not to move around the boat unnecessarily; staying on one place will minimize their chances of falling and hurting themselves.

Lightning is a serious situation you may confront when caught in bad weather. When you first notice lightning, listen for the thunder and count the seconds between the time you see the lightning and when you hear the thunder; divide this number by five to find out how far away in miles the lightning is. The chances of your being struck by lightning while on a powerboat are slim, so you don't need to be unduly afraid, but that doesn't mean you can ignore it either. Areas of lightning are usually compact and are often easy to avoid. If caught in one of these areas, stay calm, make sure you have rubber-soled shoes on, and avoid touching large metal objects on your boat.

If you're caught in bad weather and feel you may not be able to handle it, you should switch your VHF radio to channel 16 and contact the coast guard (see chapter 8). Advise them of your location and of the problems you're having. If they feel it's warranted, they'll establish what is called a *radio schedule* and will contact you at regular intervals to monitor your situation. Do not ask the coast guard to come to your boat to rescue you unless you believe your life to be in danger.

DO I NEED A COMPASS?

The only answer to this question is yes! Even if you boat only in clear weather on waters you know like the back of your hand, a *compass* provides a useful reference. (However, I'll tell you why you'll want to look at charts in the next section.) If you boat in areas where fog is a regular occurrence

Learning how to use a **compass** and up-to-date **charts** is essential. Invest in weatherproof charts if you boat frequently in a given area.

dividers

parallel rulers

hand-bearing compass

or where weather can change quickly, you absolutely need a compass—and you need to know how to use it. As electronic gear becomes more and more sophisticated, there's a tendency to rely solely on GPS (global positioning system) units and ignore the old standby of a compass and chart (see page 61 for more information about GPS units). But your boat's compass is more than a decorative item; it's a real tool that mariners since Columbus have relied on to chart courses and determine positions. You too should learn to use your compass, especially since batteries can die or fuses blow.

As you look at charts, you'll notice that they have what are called *compass roses* printed on them in various places, which help you plot courses. The compass rose gives two sets of *headings*, which are divided into 360 degrees (a *heading* is the direction in which the boat is pointing). The outer circle of degrees shows *true* headings, whereas the inner circle displays *magnetic* headings. The heading shown on your compass always correlates to the magnetic headings on a chart's compass rose. The easterly or westerly difference between true headings and magnetic headings changes from place to place and is called *local variation*. Because there are few places on earth where there is no difference between *magnetic north* and *true north*, all charts include information on the amount of variation. All compasses are affected by the Earth's natural magnetism, which is why, instead of pointing to true north, they point to magnetic north, which is a few degrees to the side. Marine charts give the amount of variance so you can make the proper corrections as you plot a course and so you can maintain the proper heading under way.

The difference between the magnetic heading shown on your compass and the magnetic heading shown on your chart's compass rose is called *deviation*. Deviation is caused by metal objects and electrical fields on your boat that can affect your compass. To determine how much deviation your compass has, plot a magnetic course between two fixed known objects on a chart, and then steer that course aboard your boat and see what your compass heading is. For example, if the course on the chart between two floating channel markers, called *buoys*, is 175 degrees and your compass reads 179 degrees as you steer in a straight line from one buoy to the other, your compass has 4 degrees of deviation. To makes things even more complicated, deviation can change depending on the direction you are going. Fortunately, you can hire a professional compass adjuster, who should be able to eliminate most of the deviation in your compass.

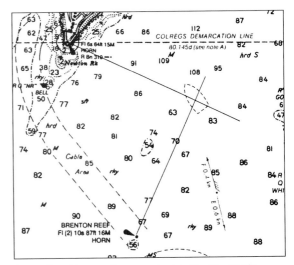

Lines of position run from your boat to fixed landmarks. By marking two lines of position on a chart, you can determine your current location.

You should learn to use your compass to determine your current position. To do this, find two known landmarks that are within sight of you, preferably about 90 degrees apart, and take *bearings* on them. Before taking these bearings, you should slow your boat down or, even better, stop it, because the bearings will change quickly if you are moving fast. To take a bearing, all you need to do is sight along your compass to see what course you would have to steer to hit the landmark in question. Taking bearings is easiest if you use a *hand-bearing compass*, which is just a handheld compass you can hold right up to your eye. Once you have your bearings, plot them on your chart, running out in straight lines from each landmark. Where the lines intersect is your location; these lines are called *lines of position*, and where they intersect is called a *fix*.

It's a good idea to get into the habit of taking fixes, especially if you're cruising in new waters. Between fixes, you should keep track of your location with *dead reckoning*. All this means is that you should be aware of the course you're steering and the approximate speed you're traveling so that you can at any time estimate where you are in relation to your last fix. Using the simple formula

Speed (in knots) × **Time** (in minutes) = **Distance** (in nautical miles)

will tell you how far along your course you've traveled.

USING CHARTS

Charts are maps of the water. Although many new powerboaters may think they aren't very useful, after you learn to read them, you'll be amazed at all the information packed onto them. Even if you've never been on a particular body of water before, charts provide all the details you'll need to navigate it like it was your backyard.

● ●

"I really don't use charts much in my home waters, but whenever I take my boat on vacation, which is a lot, the first thing I do is get a chart of the local waters to plan trips. I've used them to find out where to fish, where to scuba dive, and where I can pull in for lunch."

—Bobbi Browne, Portland, Oregon

● ●

You don't have to be a master navigator to read a chart, and you'll find the symbols on them are pretty intuitive. The most important information they contain is the depth of the water, shown in numbers called *soundings*, and the locations and identities of navigation buoys. Soundings can be in either feet or *fathoms* (a fathom is 6 feet), and each chart will note on the side which measuring system it uses. The characteristics of each buoy are expressed via abbreviations, and each chart has a key defining these abbreviations. The number or letter in quotes next to each buoy is the number or letter you will find painted on that buoy when you see it.

When using a chart, it is important to know how old it is. Each chart's date is printed on the chart, and older charts may no longer be accurate. Soundings may have changed in places with sandy, shifting bottoms, and it is very likely that some buoys will have been renumbered or moved. There also may be new breakwaters, docks, marinas, and so on that have been built since the chart was printed.

To plot a course or bearing on a chart, you'll need a tool called a *parallel ruler* (see page 58). This ruler allows you to take a line you have drawn anywhere on your chart and move it over to the compass rose to measure off your heading, or vice versa, without changing the line's angle. Note that any line drawn through a compass rose in fact has two headings, depending on which way you are going. To avoid confusion, any course you draw on a chart should have an arrow on it indicating which direction the heading relates to. The heading should be written next to the arrow with an M or T after it to indicate whether it is magnetic or true.

Distances on marine charts are in *nautical miles*. Along the edges of the chart are a series of hash marks and numbers. The increments along the sides of the chart represent minutes of *latitude*, divided into tenths. Lines of latitude are the horizontal lines around the Earth, starting with the equator, that divide it into 360 equal parts of 60 nautical miles each. There are 60 minutes to a degree, with 1 nautical mile equal to 1 minute of latitude. The increments along the top and bottom of the chart measure lines of *longitude*. These lines represent the distances between meridians of longitude that run north and south around the Earth and pass through the two poles; they're generally not used when plotting courses. Any position on the chart can be described using latitude and longitude *coordinates*.

To find the distance between two points on a chart, space out the distance with a pair of *dividers* (see page 58), and then, without changing the angle between the two points of the dividers, place the dividers over the latitude scale on the side of the chart and read off the distance in minutes. As mentioned above, each minute of latitude (not longitude!) is equal to exactly 1 nautical mile (a nautical mile is the same as 1.15 *statute*, or land, miles).

GPS UNITS AND OTHER ELECTRONIC TOOLS

Over the past several years, GPS (global positioning system) receivers have evolved from expensive navigation tools used mostly by military and commercial vessels to handy, afford-able devices that are widely used by most recreational boaters. By cross-referencing signals received from a series of different satellites, a GPS will tell you where you are, where you've been, how fast you're going, how far you've come, which way you're going, and which way you have to steer to get to a given location. I have a compass and a full set of local charts on my power-boat, but for keeping track of where I am these days, I mostly rely on a handheld GPS. Even in complete darkness, dense rain, or fog, I can "see" where I am and where I'm going.

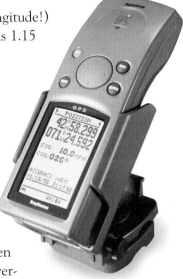

With **handheld GPS units** priced at under $200, you can equip even the smallest boat with state-of-the-art satellite navigation gear. This GPS unit gives your position in nautical coordinates; some units even offer chart displays.

Even more useful than a GPS is an *electronic chart plotter*, which will take your GPS position and automatically plot it for you on an electronic chart of the area you are in.

With all this high-tech wizardry, you may be tempted to think you don't need any paper charts or a compass and that you needn't learn any basic navigation skills. A good navigator, how-ever, uses all available sources of information to determine her position. If you rely solely on a GPS to find your way, then you'll be lost if it breaks or if the government decides for some reason to shut down the GPS satellite system (as it did briefly at the beginning of the Persian Gulf War).

It's best to use your GPS to help teach you navigation skills. For example, plot your posi-tion taking compass bearings; then check that position against the one on the GPS. Next, esti-mate the distance and course you have run from your last fix, plot a dead reckoning position, and check that against the GPS. Used wisely in this way, the GPS can make you a better, more accu-rate navigator and can help build your confi-dence without making you dependent on the GPS.

Another useful electronic tool to have on

Some GPS units can be interfaced with a laptop **chart plotter** for larger, easier to read, more detailed screen display.

board is a *depth-sounder*. The most basic ones simply tell you how much water is under your boat, which helps keep you from running your boat aground. You should always know the *draft* (depth) of any boat you're operating so you'll know how much water it needs to float. Depth-sounders can also help with navigation, because you can sometimes determine your position by checking the soundings your depth-sounder shows against those on the chart. On a foggy or rainy day, for example, when you can't see anything, you may be able to tell how far from shore you are just by knowing how deep the water is.

More advanced depth-sounders, which are marketed as *fish-finders*, display a moving picture of the bottom and also show schools of fish as they move under your boat. Additional electronic equipment you might want on your boat will include a VHF radio and perhaps even a *radar* set, which will help you navigate and avoid other vessels when visibility is poor. VHF radios and other safety gear are covered in detail in chapter 8.

TIDES AND CURRENTS

Another big factor in navigating your powerboat is knowing how the water is moving under and around your boat. Currents may be caused by many factors—including the natural flow of a river and long periods of sustained winds—and may even be permanent in nature, as with the Gulf Stream. One of the biggest causes of currents is the tide. In some areas, tides may be small or even nonexistent, but in others they can be enormous, as much as 20 feet or more.

If you aren't aware of its actions, a fast current can set you far off course or considerably increase or decrease your speed without your knowing it. This can lead to some unpleasant surprises. In some areas, tidal variations in water level will also play an important role in determining where you can and cannot take your boat. Also, when the wind blows against a strong current, the water can become very rough and uncomfortable, perhaps even dangerous. You should always be searching for clues to which way the tide or current is going and how fast it is. Look at fixed objects in the water, such as buoys, pilings, and moored boats, and see how quickly and in which direction the water is flowing past them.

Your GPS can also be a valuable tool for studying the current. For example, if your speedometer, or *log*, tells you your speed through the water is 10 *knots* (that is, 10 nautical miles per hour), and your GPS tells you it is 12 knots, you know you have 2 knots of current pushing you from behind. Or if your compass tells you you're steering a course of 110 degrees and your GPS tells you your course is 120 degrees, you know that a current is pushing you to the right. Once you know what the current or tide is doing, you can take it into account when planning your trip and navigating.

Tidal currents, at least, are very predictable. Local *tide tables* give the time for high and low tides each day as well as the height of the tide. These tables are easy to obtain at fuel docks and marine stores, and often they're printed in local newspapers. Tide charts, such as those published in *Eldridge Tide and Pilot Book* (available through Landfall Navigation, see chapter 11, Resources, as well as online bookstores), will also show you where tidal currents run strongest and weakest on the East Coast, particularly the Northeast. I use a program on my computer that provides tide and current data; by checking it before a cruise, I know what to expect. If I'm launching a boat from a trailer, I can use this information to adjust my schedule so that I launch and retrieve my boat at high tide, when doing so is easiest.

NAVIGATION AIDS

Instead of road signs, U.S. waterways have *navigation aids* called *daymarkers* and *buoys* that tell you where to go, confirm your position, and identify areas, such as rocks and shoals, that should be avoided. A *channel* is a waterway's equivalent of a highway and is delineated by daymarkers and buoys. Daymarkers are normally found in waters up to 8 to 10 feet deep and consist of signs on poles; they are not lighted. The signs are green and square or red and triangular.

> "**My** trick for staying in the middle of the channel and not running aground is to run an imaginary line from one marker to the next. Even if I'm on a section of water I've never seen before, all I need to do is keep the red ones on one side, and the greens on the other."
>
> —Cindy Davenport, Hollywood, Florida

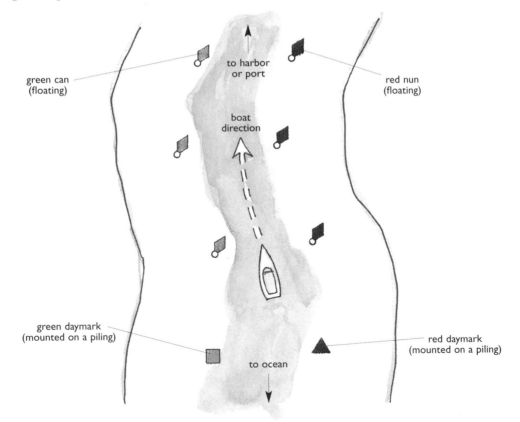

In order to keep you in the center of a channel or waterway, **navigation aids** in the form of buoys or daymarks are placed in pairs. They are normally positioned so that while you're passing one set, you can see the next set ahead.

Floating buoys are found in deeper water and are called *nuns* (red, cone-shaped buoys) or *cans* (green, cylindrical buoys); buoys can be lighted. Each marker or buoy is numbered (odd numbers for the green ones and even numbers for the red ones). A buoy with a light or sound device on it, such as a bell, gong, horn, or whistle, can be any shape.

When navigation aids are used to mark a channel, their color becomes very important. In the United States, the rule is "red right returning." This means whenever you are entering a harbor (that is, "returning" to it) or moving from a larger body of water to a smaller one (for example, from the ocean into an inlet or river), you should keep all the red buoys and markers on your right side. Conversely, when you're leaving a harbor, you should keep the green buoys on your right.

As long as you stay between the red and green markers and buoys, you know you are in the channel and won't run aground. Whenever a channel splits in two, this "fork in the road" will be marked by a buoy with red and green horizontal stripes. If the top stripe is green and the buoy is a can, leave it to port to stay in the best channel. If the top stripe is red and the buoy is a nun, leave it to starboard to stay in the best channel.

These are only the most basic aids to navigation. As you spend more time on the water and study your charts, you'll come to learn more about these and other aids and how to read them and understand all the information they provide. The most important thing, particularly when boating in an area that is new to you, is to identify each buoy or mark you see and locate it on your chart. This will help you stay out of trouble and keep track of where you are.

WHO HAS THE RIGHT-OF-WAY?

There are times when it seems like a free-for-all out on the water, with boats of all sizes and shapes apparently going wherever they please. Despite how chaotic things look, especially during times of heavy boat traffic like holiday weekends, there are in fact detailed rules about which boats have right-of-way over other boats. Anyone operating a boat must know these rules; if you don't and your ignorance causes an accident, you can be found liable and your insurance company may refuse to pay claims for damages.

We'll discuss the basic rules here, but you should also get a copy of the full U.S. Coast Guard *Navigation Rules, International–Inland,* and study them carefully (see chapter 11 for information on obtaining a copy of these rules). If you are operating a boat 39 feet or longer, you're required to carry a copy of these rules on board at all times.

The general theory behind the rules is that boats that are more maneuverable should yield to boats that are less maneuverable. The official hierarchy, from the most maneuverable on down, is

1.   Power-driven vessels (including sailboats that have their engines on)

2.   Sailboats under sail

3.   Vessels that are fishing (excluding sport or recreational fishing boats)

4. Vessels restricted in their ability to maneuver (usually working vessels, such as tugboats, towboats, and buoy tenders, that are engaged in some activity)

5. Vessels not under command (usually a vessel that isn't moored or tied up but for some special reason, such as a dead engine, cannot maneuver at all)

As you can see, as a powerboater all you have to do is remember to give way to everyone else! In many situations, you'll need to give way even to other powerboats. For example, when operating your boat in a channel or other narrow waterway, you must stay to the right-hand side and must give way to any other vessel (a large freighter, for example) that is too deep to operate outside the channel or waterway.

In a situation where one boat is passing another boat from behind, the boat that is being passed has the right-of-way, regardless of the other rules. Use your horn to let the other boat know your intentions: two toots means you will pass on the other boat's port side; one means you will pass on its starboard side. If the other boat agrees, it will acknowledge with the same signal; if not, it will sound its horn five times. If two boats are meeting head-on, there is no special right-of-way rule, but the boats should pass each other "port to port," which means they should pass to the right, each keeping the other on their port side.

Most often on the open water, boats will be coming at you, or you will be coming at them, from the side and at an angle. This is known as a *crossing situation*. To figure out

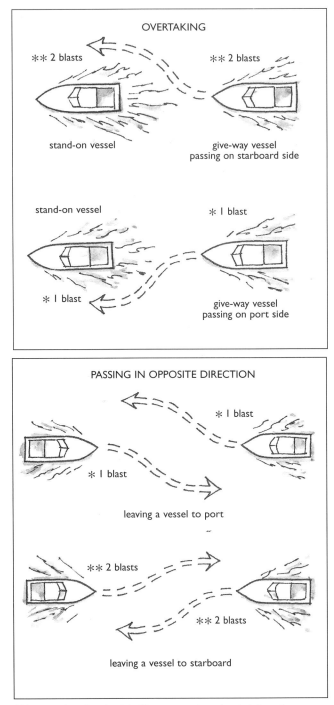

When passing other boat traffic, use your horn to alert the other vessel which side you will pass on. The other boat will respond with the same signal to affirm or sound 5 blasts to indicate dissent.

"**O**n weekends during the summer, there can be so many other boats out on the water you have to really pay attention, and the jet skis seem to pop up out of nowhere right in front of you. You can't always rely on the other boat to stay out of your way even if you know you have the right-of-way, so a lot of the time I'll change my course just to be safe."

—Danielle Vachs, Ft. Lauderdale, Florida

whether there is any chance of a collision, you should take a bearing on the other boat. You can do this with a compass, or you can just pick a reference point somewhere on your boat—such as the edge of your windshield or a particular section of handrail—and notice where the other boat is in relation to it. Keep taking bearings every few moments while maintaining your course. If the bearing changes, there is no danger of collision, but if it doesn't change, you're on a collision course.

Any time you are on a collision course with another boat in a crossing situation and that boat isn't a powerboat, you will have to yield. Usually, it's best to change course so that you pass behind the other boat. Or, you can reduce speed or even stop your boat. If the other boat is a powerboat, you must give way if it is on your starboard side, unless it is passing you from behind, in which case the rule above applies and you have the right-of-way. The area you must therefore be careful to watch, known as the *danger zone*, starts at your bow and reaches about three-quarters of the way around your boat on its starboard side. As a powerboater, you are expected to yield to any other vessel in your danger zone.

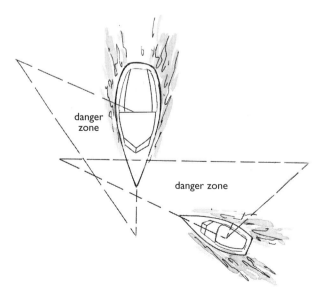

The **danger zone** of your boat starts at the bow and includes three-quarters of the starboard side. You should yield to any vessel in your danger zone.

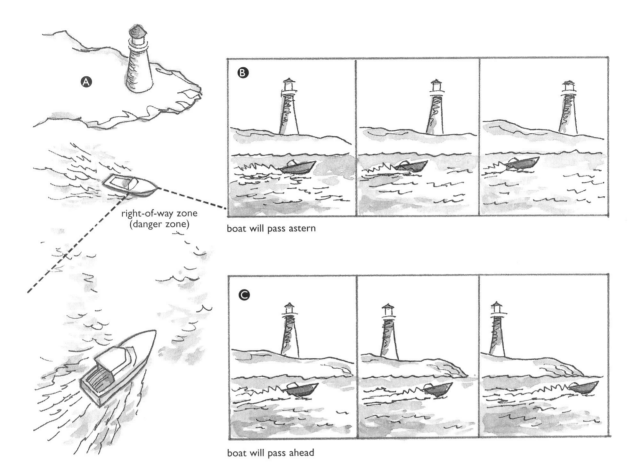

right-of-way zone (danger zone)

boat will pass astern

boat will pass ahead

A. In this typical crossing situation, you are in the other boat's **danger zone**, and it should yield to you if there is danger of a collision. To determine if you're on a collision course, pick a fixed landmark as a reference point. **B.** As both boats maintain course, if the other boat stays left in reference to the object, it will pass astern of you. **C.** If the other boat moves to the right, it will pass ahead of you. If the other boat stays in roughly the same position relative to the reference point, you are on a collision course and must alter direction immediately.

In situations where you have the right-of-way (for example, if you are in another powerboat's danger zone), your first obligation is to maintain your course and speed so as not to confuse the other boat. This is especially important when you're being passed from behind. If things start getting a little too cozy, and you're afraid the other boat won't yield, you may change your course, but under the rules you are not allowed to change course to port if the boat you're trying to avoid is on your port side. If, in a worst-case scenario, there is nothing the other boat can do to avoid you, you must take any action necessary to avoid a collision.

This may all sound confusing at first, but it starts to make a lot of sense once you gain experience. The most important thing is to keep a good eye out for other boats and always be ready to yield, even if you think you have the right-of-way.

LIGHTS AT NIGHT

Boating at night involves an entirely new set of sensations; sounds travel farther, the stars seem close enough to touch, and the air is usually cooler. But your visibility is greatly decreased, and it can be very hard to judge distance accurately, so you need to exercise much more caution.

All boats are supposed to have a set of *navigation lights*, which allow you not only to spot them easily from a distance but also determine what type of boat they are and in which direction they are traveling. All powerboats 39 feet and longer are required to have one white light, known as a *masthead light*, mounted upright and facing forward in the center of the boat and visible through an arc of 225 degrees, as well as another white light (called a *stern light*) mounted at the stern and facing aft. Power vessels longer than 164 feet must have two masthead lights, and powerboats shorter than 39 feet may show one all-around white light instead of a masthead light and stern light.

In addition to their white lights, every powerboat must have *sidelights*, which are red and green lights shown on the port and starboard sides respectively. Together, the sidelights must be visible through the same 225-degree forward arc as is the masthead light.

With a little practice, you'll be able to discern quickly how other boats are oriented with respect to you at night. For example, if you see a red light with a white light over it, you know you are looking at the front port side of a powerboat. If you see a red and a green light side by side with a white light over them, you are looking at the front of a powerboat coming directly at you. If you see just a white light, you are looking at the stern of a powerboat.

There are many other rules pertaining to lights shown on other types of boats, such as working fishing boats, towboats, sailboats (which must show the same lights as powerboats when using

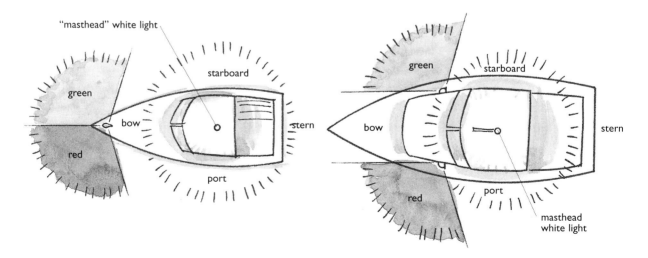

No matter how large or small a boat may be, it must have a white light to show it's under power, as well as red and green lights to indicate its port and starboard sides. As the size of the boat increases, the location of these lights on the boat may change, but the colors and their meaning remain the same.

their engines, but different lights when sailing), and even submarines and seaplanes. If you are going to spend much time on the water at night, study the Navigation Rules carefully. You will also need to study the different sorts of lights shown on different navigation aids and buoys. Especially if you're boating someplace with lots of background lights on shore, it can take some practice before you can quickly distinguish among different lights. Always be extra cautious when boating at night!

SPEED LIMITS

One of the more enjoyable aspects of power-boating is going fast. But how fast should you go? Generally, if there are speed limits, there

Aids to navigation include information and regulatory signs that warn of special restrictions, shallow areas, and other hazards. A red crossed diamond indicates an exclusion area; a red circle indicates restricted operations, such as speed limits; a red diamond indicates danger.

will be signs telling you the maximum speed for that area. Often you will see an *idle-speed zone* or a *no-wake zone*, where you are required to go slow enough to keep your powerboat's wake to a minimum. These zones are common in areas of restricted maneuverability or where a large wake could damage seawalls or wildlife on the banks of the shore.

There's no doubt that driving a powerboat fast is a major thrill, and this is one of the reasons a lot of us choose to be powerboaters. But the thrill comes with the need to be a responsible boater. Even if you're in an area with no speed limits, you still need to exercise common sense. One of the most important Navigation Rules is that you must maintain a safe speed "appropriate to the prevailing circumstances and conditions." Thus, you should take into consideration such factors as how much traffic there is, how big the waves are, how far you can see, how deep the water is, and how close you are to any dangers.

Keep in mind that driving a speeding boat is much different from driving a car. There are no seatbelts on a powerboat, and if you hit a large wave, you could lose control of the boat or be knocked completely out of it. You may have the steering wheel to hang onto, but your passengers might not have anything to hold them in place. Have fun, but make sure you are in an area where it's both legal and safe to go fast, tell your passengers to hold on tight, and keep an eye out for other boats.

Don't *ever* try to pass another boat by zooming past it; besides being rude, it's dangerous and can earn you a ticket if a marine law enforcement officer sees you do it. Time on the water is supposed to be fun, so try cruising along and taking the time to enjoy the scenery—you might discover it's more enjoyable to go slow and stately than to blast along in a big hurry.

Chapter 6

ESSENTIAL EQUIPMENT

As you spend more time on the water, you'll quickly devise your own list of essential equipment, ranging from a hypoallergenic sunblock to a handheld VHF radio. The idea is not to bring everything you could possibly need, but rather to learn which things make each cruise more enjoyable and safer.

In addition to the safety equipment required by the U.S. Coast Guard (see Required Safety and Emergency Equipment, page 97), some basics you can't go wrong on are enough drinking water and juice for everyone, a cellular phone, light snacks, a comprehensive first-aid kit, a camera to record the memories, and a credit card for anything you forgot.

BOAT-BUYING BASICS

With so many types of boats available, how do you pick the right one? For me, it comes down to three issues: what is your "dream boat," can you afford it, and how often will you realistically be able to use it? If your ideal boat is larger than your budget, you will need to scale back to a choice that is within your means. Even if you can afford a large boat, however, ask yourself whether you would be more likely to use a smaller vessel.

For instance, although you might be able to afford a 30-foot express cruiser that you keep docked at a marina and that requires an hour to get ready to go cruising, it may be you would actually get a lot more use from a 15-foot center console that you keep on a trailer at home and can have in the water and ready to go in 20 minutes. If you make a mistake and end up with the wrong boat, you can always sell it and start over. Speaking as someone who has found herself doing exactly that, however, I can honestly say that taking an hour or so for soul-searching during the decision-making process can save you a lot of headaches later.

The next question is, where do you buy a boat? Boats are available wherever there's water as well as a lot of places without water. You can shop for powerboats at marinas, boat dealers, and boat shows; through classified ads in magazines and local papers; and even over the Internet. Purchasing a boat is an exciting event, but it can be confusing too, so it's a good idea to shop with a friend who can help you sort out the details later. Don't be afraid to take notes, and do ask lots of questions. Purchasing your own powerboat is a big step, but it can also be the first step to a whole new life—despite all the responsibilities that go with boat ownership, I wouldn't be without one.

CHOOSING BETWEEN A NEW AND A USED BOAT

Once you've decided on the make and model of powerboat you want, the question becomes, should you buy new or used? Each type has certain advantages, and the decision really comes down to what makes you comfortable.

New boats normally come with a warranty, so if a problem arises, the dealer or manufacturer will take care of it. New boats have never been abused, run aground, or otherwise damaged. But all that shiny newness can be reflected in the purchase price.

Your other alternative is to buy a used boat. Because boats depreciate at least as much as most cars do, by choosing a model that's a year or more older, you can save a significant amount of money. Few boatowners use their boats as often as they had originally planned, and the result is many slightly used boats for sale. Add to this availability the fact that many boat models don't change significantly from year to year, which means you can still get the model you want while saving a large amount of money by choosing a used version. However, buying used has its downside,

REGISTERING YOUR BOAT

• • • • • • • • • • • • • • • • • •

As with cars, powerboats must be registered with the state in which you live on an annual basis. Fees vary from state to state, and usually reflect the size of the boat—the larger the boat, the more expensive the registration fee. Registered boats bear identification numbers and letters on either side of the bow, starting with a two-letter prefix to identify the home state (e.g., *FL* for Florida).

In most states, no matter how small the boat may be, if it has an engine, it must be registered. The only boats that aren't state registered are larger boats that are instead *documented* by the U.S. Coast Guard. Registration is usually just a matter of remitting the annual fee, receiving and affixing an annual decal that's usually displayed near the state registration numbers—there are usually no state-required inspections in order to register powerboats. Annual renewals can be as simple as paying the fee and attaching the new registration decal.

If the powerboat has a trailer, it too must be registered each year; inspection requirements vary for trailers.

(continued on next page)

REGISTERING YOUR BOAT

• • • • • • • • • • • • • • • • • • •

(continued from previous page)
Remember that requirements vary from state to state, so make sure you get the information you need about your state, and make sure you understand it.

too. The biggest hurdle is making sure you get your dream boat instead of someone else's floating nightmare. Remember this: if it's such a great boat, ask the seller why it's for sale. Listen carefully to the answer to see whether it makes sense.

Once you make the decision to purchase a particular used boat, a relatively easy way to avoid problems is to have a marine surveyor inspect the boat prior to your buying it. Because the cost of a surveyor will start at around $300 and increase with the size of the boat being inspected, this is a step that should be taken only if you're serious about this particular powerboat.

A surveyor will inspect every inch of the boat and all its equipment and then provide a detailed report of the findings. A survey is the fastest way to determine the condition of a particular boat, as well as what it could cost to repair any defects that may have been discovered. As a bonus, a competent surveyor will also include in the report a market-value estimate, which will give you an idea as to whether you've got a bargain or an overinflated asking price. Although there are no state or federal regulations or requirements governing surveyors, the two professional associations surveyors can join in order to be certified are NAMS (the National Association of Marine Surveyors) and SAMS (the Society of Marine Surveyors). Both groups will provide the names of surveyors in your area.

So what's the answer to the new or used question? It really depends on the boat and how you feel about it. I've bought brand-new boats and others that were several years old when I purchased them. Except for one purchase I rushed into, I've been happy with all of them. The buying process is supposed to be fun, so take your time and enjoy it. Most importantly, if you have any doubts, don't be afraid to pass on a deal. The one thing I can promise is that there will almost always be another "great deal" just down the road.

WHAT YOU REALLY NEED ON BOARD

In addition to knowing how to operate a powerboat safely, you can help ensure an enjoyable day out on the water by having the right gear on your boat. To me, essential gear includes the right clothes, basic safety and communications equipment, and any-

Waterproof bags are available in a variety of shapes and sizes to keep your personal belongings dry and safe.

thing else I may need to be comfortable while I'm out on the boat.

After a while, you'll realize there are certain items you tend to bring with you for a day of boating. Safety gear, discussed in detail in chapter 8, is absolutely on the list. For me, basic essential gear includes a medical emergency kit, sunblock, a handheld VHF radio, a compass, a GPS unit, a compact air horn for signaling, pocket flares, a waterproof flashlight, spare batteries, a Leatherman multitool device, and a small roll of shrink-wrap tape. Shrink-wrap tape is the boater's version of duct tape and is superior because it doesn't leave a messy residue. It's handy to patch holes in upholstery or foul-weather gear, temporarily fix broken pipes and hoses, and just generally hold things in place.

My basic gear always goes with me, whether I'm on my own boat or doing a boat test for a magazine, so I store it in a waterproof nylon duffel bag. Full, it weighs about 10 pounds and goes straight from the shelf in my garage to the boat. Because it's easy to overdo it when packing a bag, I weighed mine to prevent going over 10 pounds. If the bag is too heavy to move easily, you won't bring it, which defeats the purpose.

BOAT RENTALS

Many people opt to rent boats because purchasing a boat is only the beginning of a larger responsibility that includes having to insure, store, and maintain it. If you're relatively new to boating, it can be helpful to rent several different boats to get an idea of what features you like—or need—and certainly also whether you want to take the next step and purchase your own boat.

Most waterfront areas have local firms that rent powerboats by the hour, half day, or full day, without the requirement of a club membership. Club Nautico is a boat rental organization with a wide variety of types and sizes of powerboats for use on inland or coastal waters around the United States, though most of its offices are in Florida (see chapter 11, Resources, for contact information). I'm not aware of any companies that currently offer long-term leases on boats, so renting or purchasing are the only viable options at present.

A NOTE ABOUT CELLULAR PHONES

. . . .

Cellular phones are the best way to stay in touch with those on land and can also be used to call other cellular-equipped powerboats. But because they are not designed to serve the needs of those on the water, don't rely on one as your sole means of communication while afloat. If you do need to use one in the event of an emergency, simply dial 911 and advise the operator you're on a boat; you'll be connected with the coast guard or other appropriate party.

COMMUNICATION AFLOAT: WHY YOU NEED A VHF RADIO

I discuss VHF radios and their use at length in chapter 8, but here is a quick overview. A VHF radio is your best means of staying in communication with other boaters, with persons on shore (such as at marinas), or with emergency assistance organizations (such as the coast guard).

A VHF radio is better than a cellular phone for contacting other boats; you don't need to know specific phone numbers because every boat with a VHF radio will hear your message. There's room on even the smallest powerboat for a handheld VHF radio; I use a handheld model made by Uniden that is compact, completely waterproof, and affordable at less than $200. Even if you don't actively listen to every transmission on the radio, while you're on the boat and under way, leave it turned on and set to channel 16 so you can hear any emergency messages or weather alerts.

TOOLS AND SPARE PARTS

The majority of the time, your powerboating experience will consist of time spent on the water with friends, enjoying the sensation of the boat, the sun, and the fresh breeze as you watch the scenery roll past. However, because a powerboat is a mechanical object, no matter how reliable it is and how well you maintain it, every once in a while something will need to be adjusted, repaired, or replaced.

When you're on the water, you also have to be prepared to take care of yourself and your passengers. By staying in the center of marked channels, watching out for low bridges or trash floating in the water, and keeping an eye on fuel and oil levels, you can easily avoid a lot of problems. But in the event something does happen, simply being prepared for it goes a long way toward surviving the ordeal. The most common mechanical problems are drained batteries, running out of fuel, and bending a propeller. In these situations, there isn't much you can do on your own other than call a marine assistance and towing company, such as Sea Tow, on your VHF.

But if all that happens is a screw coming loose, your propeller becoming tangled in a clump of fishing line, or one of your navigation light's bulbs burning out, a few simple tools can have you back in action quickly. I carry a small tool kit that includes a wrench, several screwdrivers, and pliers. If I can't fix the problem with these tools, I call for help. If I'm a guest on someone's powerboat, instead of the tool kit I carry a SOG PowerPlier in my equipment bag. This compact multitool device combines pliers with screwdrivers and is big enough to be really useful, yet it's compact enough to be carried easily. Mine has a gold-titanium-nitride finish, making it highly resistant to corrosion.

I also always carry a good-quality knife in my boater's bag in case I need to cut a tangle of fishing line from a propeller. I've relied on a Spyderco Mariner for many years to do everything from cutting a tangled anchor line to trimming the crust off sandwiches. The serrated blade is great for cutting quickly through even the heaviest materials, and because it's stainless, it's easy to keep clean and rust free.

As far as spare parts go, some people advise carrying one of everything, but on my powerboat, that wouldn't leave room for me and my passengers. Modern powerboats are very reliable and unlikely to break down; if they do, chances are it's something beyond the average powerboater's abilities to fix unless she happens to be a master mechanic. The things most likely to break are usually small and easy to replace, such as bulbs, hose clamps, screws, or loose wires, and a small supply of these parts will cost under $10 and fit in a very small bag that's easily tucked away. I carry a spare propeller and a prop wrench and suggest that you do, too, but beyond these few spare parts and a basic tool kit, that's it.

ANCHORS AND ANCHORING

The purpose of an anchor is to hold the boat in one place. Many powerboaters go for years without ever using their anchors, but it's one piece of equipment for which there is no substitute. The most common types of anchor systems are the *twin fluke* (examples of common brands are Danforth, Fortress, and West), which has two sharp-edge "flukes" that pivot away from a straight arm, or *stock*, to provide a solid hold in sandy or muddy bottoms; the *plow*, which digs into the bottom like a farmer's plow and is well

MAKING INFORMED EQUIPMENT PURCHASES

• • • • • • • • • • • • • • • •

Because only an informed buyer can make the best purchase decisions, when it comes time to purchase marine equipment, check current boating magazines for reviews of the gear you're considering. At *Boating* magazine, I review many types of boating equipment for our We Test section, where we offer our impressions of how the gear functions and tell how to get further information. Most boating magazines have similar features or departments, so read up!

TOOL KIT

• • • • • • • • • • • • • • • • • •

The basic tool kit on any powerboat should contain at least the following.

- shrink-wrap tape
- electrical tape
- electric circuit tester
- flashlight with spare batteries and bulbs
- hex keys
- knife
- pliers
- propeller wrench
- several screwdrivers (slot head and Phillips)
- spare impeller (part of the water-cooling mechanism on outboard engines)
- spare propeller
- spare spark plug
- spark plug wrench

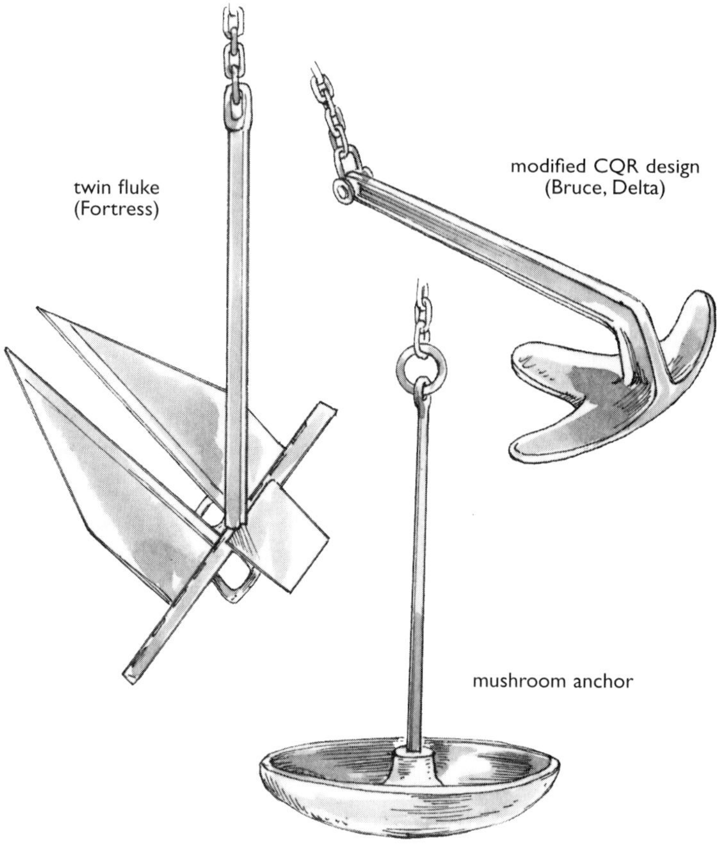

twin fluke
(Fortress)

modified CQR design
(Bruce, Delta)

mushroom anchor

There are many types of **anchors** because each is designed to work on a specific type of bottom, such as a sandy bottom or a rocky bottom.

suited for rocky or grassy bottoms (CQR); one-piece variations of the plow (Bruce and Delta); and the *mushroom*, which looks a lot like an upside-down mushroom and is used by smaller boats (less than 25 feet) in sand or mud bottoms. Large mushroom anchors are also used to set moorings for boats.

No matter which type of anchor you use, you'll also need an *anchor rode*, which is the line or chain that connects the anchor to the boat. The most common arrangement is for the first 20 feet of the rode to be a chain, followed by 100 or more feet of line. The weight of the chain holds the anchor in the best position for grabbing the bottom. As an added benefit, on rocky bottoms the chain won't fray or be cut the way a nylon anchor line might be.

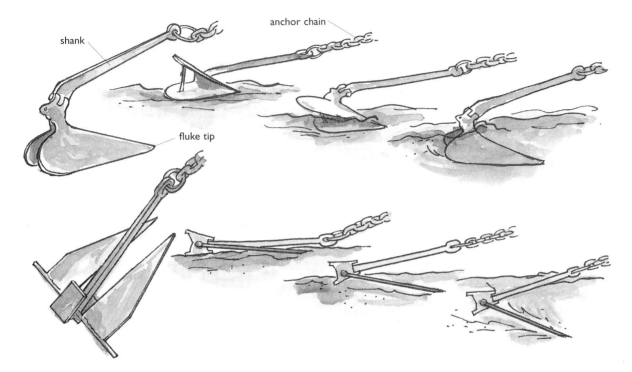

shank

anchor chain

fluke tip

An anchor holds your boat in place by digging itself into the bottom. To do this, the pull of the rode on the anchor must be horizontal, or nearly so. Increasing the length of the rode increases its scope and makes the pull on the anchor more horizontal.

Anchors come in many shapes, sizes, and materials. When choosing one for your power-boat, ask your boat dealer for advice, or go to your local West Marine store and read their *Guide to Anchors,* which includes a chart that matches your boat size with bottom types and recommends the best anchor style to match.

Using your anchor is simple. Find a place to anchor that isn't too deep for your anchor line and that isn't overly rocky—sandy or muddy bottoms work best. When you're stopped in the area you want to anchor, first make sure the anchor rode is loosely coiled with no kinks or knots in it; next gently lower the anchor over the side and let it sink to the bottom. Using a pair of lightweight gloves to guide the rode will prevent the line from burning your hands. You'll know when the anchor hits bottom because the line will stop running through your hands.

One word of caution: before you toss the anchor over the side—and after first making sure the rode runs *under* the bow rail as opposed to *over* it, where it could be bent—make sure the other end of the anchor rode is secured to your powerboat. It's very sad to watch the last of the anchor rode flutter out of sight into the depths below after you realize it wasn't connected to the boat!

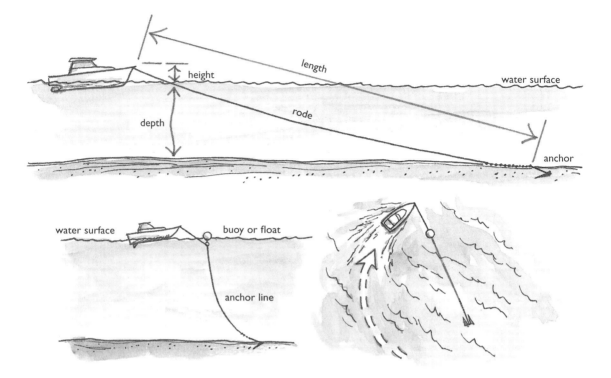

Top: Determine how much **scope** you need when anchoring based on what you know of wind and sea conditions, seabottom, and your anchor type. Add water depth, bow height, and tide height, and then multiply the sum by the amount of scope you want, to determine how much line to let out. **Bottom:** A good way to **retrieve an anchor** that won't come loose is by using a float attached to the anchor line with a stainless steel ring. When you're ready to weigh anchor, slowly driving the boat in wide circles around the anchor will cause the float to pull the anchor free of the bottom and up into the ring, where you can easily retrieve it.

Once the anchor has hit bottom, slowly back the boat up while letting out more anchor rode. Cleat the rode (see pages 49 and 51) and keep backing up slowly. As the anchor digs in, or *sets*, the boat will come to a stop and the rode will become taut. It might take a few tries, especially if there's grass on the bottom, but keep at it. While you're at anchor, periodically check to make sure the anchor hasn't come loose and started dragging across the bottom.

But how much rode should you let out when anchoring? That depends on a number of factors. The ratio of length of rode to the vertical distance to the bottom of the seabed is called *scope* (see top drawing, above). Recommended scope varies according to your anchor type's ability to hold in whatever type of seabottom you're anchoring in, given wind and sea conditions. In general, however, appropriate scope varies from about 5:1 in calm conditions to 10:1 in severe conditions, with 7:1 about normal. For example, if you've determined that you'll need a scope of 5:1 and you're anchoring in 12 feet of water, with the bow 4 feet above the surface and 1 foot of tide expected, you'll need to let out 85 feet of anchor rode.

(12 feet water depth + 4 feet bow height + 1 foot tide) × 5 = 85 feet

When you're ready to continue your cruise, prepare to raise the anchor. Instead of pulling the boat toward the anchor, drive the boat toward the anchor while a passenger takes up the anchor rode. When you're directly over the anchor, a sharp heave should break it free and allow you to pull it up to the boat. If the anchor won't come up, it might be snagged on the bottom, so take up any slack in the anchor line, secure it to the bow cleat, and slowly drive the boat in a wide circle. This should pull the anchor over to the side and break it free from the bottom so you can retrieve it.

CLOTHING FOR COMFORTABLE POWERBOATING

Dressing for a day out on the water is remarkably similar to dressing for a backyard barbeque, except that on a powerboat you need to wear shoes with a good grip and be prepared in case the weather turns windy or wet. Here's a list of clothing and gear that will let you get the most out of your boating adventures.

Boat shoes

The reasons the majority of powerboaters wear boat shoes are simple: they're comfortable, they provide secure footing even when the deck is wet, and they won't leave scuff marks on a deck the way hard-soled shoes will. The traditional boat shoe has a leather or canvas upper, but boat shoes are also available in both athletic shoe and sandal designs. The two brands I normally wear are Sperry Top-Sider and Shoes For Crews. I've found these shoes provide great arch support and stable footing on the wettest decks, and they always look good enough to wear to a waterfront restaurant.

You can buy less expensive shoes, but I've learned over the years that the bargain shoes aren't as comfortable or as durable as the brand names. The secret is the materials used. The soles should be made of white, nonscuffing rubber with grooves to allow water to sluice out (this is how they keep you from slipping on wet decks). The uppers should be securely stitched so they'll last for several seasons of wear and should have strong leather or nylon laces. Sandals with nonskid soles are popular with some women powerboaters, but I don't recommend them because they don't cover and protect your toes; all it takes is stubbing your toes once on an exposed bow cleat to understand how important this consideration is.

Warm-weather clothing

To dress right for warm-weather powerboating, dress for a picnic, choosing clothes that are light and comfortable and let you move easily. Hook & Tackle Outfitters and Columbia Sportswear both make casual clothing for women that looks as good as it works. I wear Hook & Tackle canvas cotton shorts and shirts for casual days out on the water; one style has a side pocket that holds a cellular phone or a soda can. For warm evening trips to a waterfront restaurant, I usually wear a pair of Columbia shorts; they look presentable in almost any waterfront setting while being comfortable enough for a five-hour cruise.

Top: The most effective UV blockers available are long sleeves, long pants, a hat, and sunglasses. **Bottom:** Casual clothing is the order of the day for time spent on your boat.

T-shirts are great on warm days, but make sure you protect any exposed skin with sunblock. Columbia also makes lightweight long-sleeved shirts that protect your skin from sunburn on sunny days. Features to look for in shorts include zippered pockets. (No matter how many pockets you have, however, it's a better idea to put your house and car keys, wallet, and cellular phone in a small waterproof duffel bag and store it in one of the boat's waterproof lockers.)

Sunblock and lip balm

There's nothing fashionable about being sunburned, especially since it can lead to premature aging of your skin or possibly even skin cancer. Because the drying effects of the sun are accentuated out on the water, always use lip balm and a sunblock with a high SPF to protect any exposed skin. Reapply both regularly throughout the day. After a day out on the water, it's also a good idea to clean and moisturize your skin. And don't forget your hair—use a moisturizing conditioner to help prevent split ends.

Cold-weather clothing

Unless you live in a northern state where the water freezes up, just because it starts getting colder doesn't mean you can't take the boat out. During fall in Florida, I bring along sweatshirts that are easy to pull on over a T-shirt, and when it begins to get cold, I start wearing long-sleeved shirts, khaki slacks, and fleece-lined windbreakers.

Even if it's just cool on shore, it can feel a lot colder out on the water, so a windbreaker or fleece pullover comes in handy. My favorite is the official Lifeguard windbreaker-style jacket made by Thousand Mile. Windbreakers are versatile because they're warm all by themselves or can be worn over a sweater. Stearns makes a Float Coat, which combines a windbreaker design with life-jacket flotation—I wear mine during cool months when a PFD is just too bulky to wear over a jacket. On shore I wear jeans quite often, but I normally don't wear them on the boat because they don't let me move as easily as khakis, and if they get wet, they stay damp and uncomfortable for hours.

Hat

A hat with a brim to shade your face from the harmful effects of the sun is a must, no matter what the temperature. Baseball-style caps are the most popular among powerboaters simply because they stay on. Big floppy hats may look nice and provide a lot more shade, but on a powerboat they'll quickly be blown off. After you've lost several floppy straw hats or those wide-brimmed hats you see worn on sailboats, you'll make the switch to baseball caps, too. I have long hair, so I tuck it into the back of the baseball cap to keep it from flying around and tangling. Visors are another option, but because they don't protect the top of your head, they won't keep you as cool.

If you're dressed properly, even a brisk day on the water can be fun!

Sunglasses

The sun's glare reflecting off the water can make it hard to see where you're going and can even cause damage to your eyes, so good sunglasses are essential. Choose a pair that has UV-blocking lenses that completely cover your eyes. In addition to shielding your eyes from the sun, sunglasses also protect your eyes from flying bugs and water spray, so consider a pair with wraparound lenses. My favorite sunglasses are those made by Costa Del Mar with blue reflective lenses, which block even the fiercest glare, and a neck strap, which keeps me from losing them. If you wear prescription glasses, consider getting either a pair of prescription sunglasses or a pair of glasses with Transitions lenses that darken when they're exposed to sunlight.

It isn't all that unusual to have a small bug or other foreign object fly into your eye while you're on the boat, so remember to tuck a bottle of eyewash into your boater's bag. And if you wear contact lenses, carry your glasses or a spare set of contact lenses in case you lose a lens.

Foul-weather gear

Foul-weather gear is the marine term for rain gear. Although it may seem unnecessary to many new powerboaters who intend to go out only in clear weather, they soon find out that weather changes quickly out on the water. A squall can come up from nowhere, drenching you and then blowing away to leave you in bright sunshine. And as hard as it may be to believe, many powerboaters actually like being out in a light rain. For me, it's one of the most relaxing times on the water; everything is cloaked in a fine mist, I can feel the temperature drop, and best of all, I have the waterway mostly to myself since everyone else heads back to the dock. Being out in a thunderstorm doesn't have the same charm, but if you're prepared for it with at least a well-made foul-weather jacket, playing in the rain on the boat is as much fun as it was when you were a kid playing in the puddles.

The secret is to be dressed for the weather. I wear a foul-weather jacket and bib overalls from West Marine; they fit me just right, they're lined to keep from getting clammy, and the jacket has banded sleeves and a roll-away hood in case it gets really wet out there. Douglas Gill also makes foul-weather gear in sizes to fit most women. Because the fit is important, try the clothing on before you leave the store. Add a pair of scuba diver's insulated gloves and you'll keep your hands warm while not losing any dexterity needed to run the boat.

It doesn't have to be pouring rain for you to get into your "foulies." A wet spray can quickly cool you down until you become chilled, and one of the most important tasks of foul-weather gear is to block the wind and spray. And don't forget your feet: because wet, cold feet are one of the surest ways to make you feel miserable, when it's rainy, windy, and cold out on the water, a good pair of ocean boots not only provides sure footing on a slippery deck but also keeps your feet warm and dry.

A good-quality foul-weather outfit of jacket and pants can cost about $200, and the boots about $30, but this is one outfit that will keep you comfortable for years. While you're outfitting your boat with PFDs and other safety gear, buy one or two inexpensive rain suits to keep your unprepared guests dry and comfortable.

Chapter 7

TRAILERING YOUR POWERBOAT

You don't have to live in Aspen to ski, and you don't have to live alongside a river, lake, or canal in order to enjoy powerboating. Although boats of all sizes can be transported on trailers, I recommend starting with a smaller boat (between 15 and 21 feet) because it's much easier to tow, and no matter how small you are, you can handle it.

The weight of the boat and whether your car or truck is up to the job of towing it determine whether a boat can be trailered. In general, the smaller the boat, the lighter its weight, so the easier it will be to maneuver on its trailer. Before you attempt to tow any trailer, you need to make sure your tow vehicle is up to the task by checking the weight limit for towing. Exceeding your vehicle's towing capacity could seriously damage the brakes, cooling system, or even the engine itself, so don't take a chance.

At first glance, towing a boat and launching it from a ramp seem complicated and daunting tasks, but with a little practice they quickly become just another routine stage in enjoying time on the water. Because you can take your boat almost anywhere, it's easier to take the sport with you, exploring new waters that otherwise may not be accessible or may be too far away to reach by boat alone. As a bonus, storing your boat on a trailer is normally much less expensive than keeping it in the water, and it definitely reduces such maintenance requirements as needing to apply a fresh coat of antifouling bottom paint each year.

Top: A boat stored on a trailer doesn't require costly bottom painting each season, and an unpainted bottom produces less friction, which in turn produces greater speed while requiring less fuel. **Bottom:** The parts of a trailer.

TRAILER ANATOMY

I like to think of the trailer as a boat holder with wheels. Its purpose is to give you a place to store the boat and to make it easy to get the boat to and from the water. Trailers come in a variety of shapes and sizes, each uniquely designed to carry a specific boat. This is definitely one area where one size does not fit all, so if you buy the trailer separately from the boat, make sure it's the right size. Each of the main parts involved with a trailer system is described below.

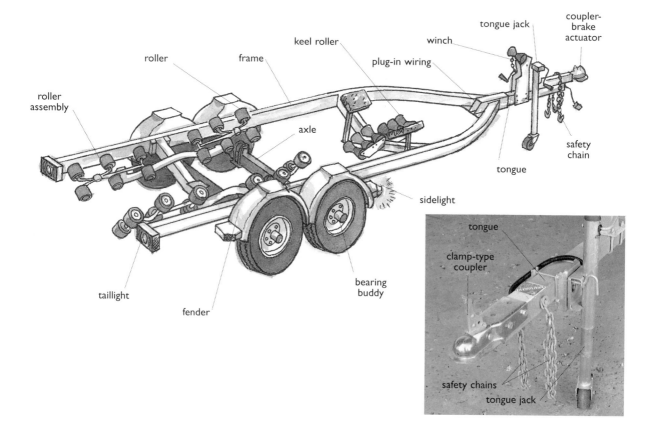

"I always go to the same coastal village on vacation, but after 12 years of going there, I finally brought my boat. I was amazed that, after vacationing at the same place for so long, how it looked so completely different from the water, and how easy it was to tow my boat. Now I plan all my vacations around the boat."

—Bonnie McArdle, Newport News, Virginia

Hitch

Before you can hook up the trailer, you need a tow vehicle that is equipped with a trailer *hitch* securely bolted or welded to the tow vehicle's frame. There are four categories of hitches, each designed for a specific weight and length of boat. Class 2 through class 4 hitches are called *receiver-style hitches* because the tubelike section of the hitch ball slides into the "receiver," which is bolted or welded to the tow vehicle's frame. Many new power-boaters start with smaller boats (15 to 21 feet) that require either a class 1 or class 2 hitch.

Hitch ball

The next step for any style of hitch system is to choose the right *hitch ball*, which needs to be rated for the weight of the boat and trailer and must also fit correctly to allow the trailer to follow the tow vehicle freely without being so loose it comes off. Hitch balls come in sizes ranging from $1\frac{7}{8}$ to $2\frac{5}{16}$ inches. Boats up to about 25 feet long require either a $1\frac{7}{8}$-inch or a 2-inch ball.

The ball has a *shank*, which functions like a bolt to hold the ball in the hitch. Just as the ball must be the right size, the shank size also needs to fit the hitch. It's easy to tell whether the shank is the right size simply by making sure it has the same diameter as the hole it fits into on the hitch. If you plan to tow the boat more than 25 miles, before lowering the trailer tongue over the hitch ball, spread a thin film of lubricant over the hitch

FIRST-TIME TRAILERING

"The first time I towed a boat by myself was the day I bought my first boat that came with a trailer, a 17-foot Boston Whaler. I went no faster than 20 miles per hour the whole way, constantly glancing at my rearview mirrors to make sure the boat was still there, with my heart pounding every time I hit a bump in the road and felt the boat trailer bounce. After the longest drive of my life, I managed to get to the boat ramp OK, but when I tried backing the car and trailer to the water's edge, the trailer suddenly veered off to the side at a 90-degree angle, and no matter what I did, it kept getting worse. Luckily, a family who had just finished launching their 21-foot bowrider came to my rescue.

"After first unclipping the *transom tie-down* holding the back of the boat to the trailer and unhooking the trailer lights from the car lights to prevent the cool water from popping the bulbs, the wife told me how to pull forward until the trailer was straight behind the car and then how to look over my right shoulder as I slowly reversed down the ramp, steering the wheel in the opposite direction I wanted

(continued on next page)

FIRST-TIME TRAILERING

• •

(continued from previous page) the trailer to go. It took a few tries, but suddenly I got the hang of it and could make the trailer go where I needed it to. Her husband and daughter positioned themselves at the water's edge to help me gauge how far to back the boat, motioning me to stop and set my parking brake when the boat started to float above the trailer's bunks.

"Before they let me float the boat free, they told me how to retrieve the boat, explaining how I'd need to line the boat up squarely over the bunks so it would rest securely on the trailer, and then how to winch it up onto the trailer and make sure it was secure by reattaching the transom tie-down, hooking up the trailer lights, and snubbing the winch line. Now when the boat starts to veer off at a sudden angle when I'm backing the boat into the water or storing it in my back yard, I know to stop, pull forward to straighten out, and start again—slowly."

—Cindy Ferrantelli,
Fort Lauderdale, Florida

Above: Receiver-style hitches let you change ball size to match any trailer you may want to tow. Left: Some hitches come with a variety of ball sizes that can be rotated for the correct size to fit almost any trailer.

ball to help it turn smoothly and keep it from overheating.

Tongue and coupler

Now that you have a hitch matched with the correct size hitch ball for the trailer tongue, let's look at the trailer itself. The part of the trailer that connects to the tow vehicle is called the *tongue*, and the device at the end of the tongue is called the *coupler*. When the coupler is lowered over the hitch ball, you either flip the *coupler clamp* down to lock it onto the hitch ball or, if using a screw-type coupler, turn the screw until it's tight. With a clamp-style coupler, it's a good idea to secure it in the locked position by inserting a padlock through the hole on the back of the clamp; this will keep the coupler from popping loose and will also keep the trailer from being stolen while you're out on the boat.

Winch

Behind the coupler is a *winch* with a steel cable that is used both to pull the boat out of the water and up onto the trailer and to help hold the boat on the trailer. (Instead of a cable, some

"The best Christmas present I ever got myself was an electric winch for my boat trailer."

—Tamara Johnson, Salt Lake City, Utah

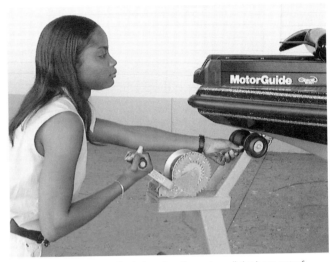

Even a one-speed **manual winch** makes it easy to pull the boat out of the water and back onto a trailer.

winches have a nylon strap, which is just as strong but won't rust or shred like a cable can.) The cable has an aluminum hook on the end that snaps into the U-shaped *bow eye*, which extends from the front of your boat just above the boat's waterline.

Winches are simple to use, and most have a high and a low gear, so even a petite woman can use one. Unless you have a small trailer with the handle permanently mounted, the winch will have a switch that lets you change the gear. Electric winches, which require simply attaching a cable and pressing a button, are the easiest to use and are best for larger and heavier boats.

A manual winch will have a stubby lever extending from one side. This lever changes the direction the winch turns, so you can use it either to let the cable out to launch the boat or to take up the cable as you pull the boat up onto the trailer. If removable, the handle can fit into one of two slots, which are high and low gear. Switching to a lower gear makes it easier to crank the winch handle.

If your trailer has a black rubber V or roller just below the winch, replace it with one made of amber-colored plastic; black rubber parts don't last as long as amber ones, and they also leave hard-to-remove scuff marks. Also consider this switch for the rollers, discussed next.

Bunks and rollers

Once on the trailer, the boat rests on *bunks* or *rollers*. Bunks are simply pieces of wood covered by carpeting, whereas rollers resemble upended roller blades with black or amber-colored wheels.

"I only weigh about 105 pounds, so I had a tough time winching my 23-foot boat onto its trailer bunks. But after I replaced the bunks with rollers, it was like the boat was on ball bearings."

—Meghan Sharkey, San Diego, California

Bunks provide the most secure resting place for a boat but require more effort to slide the boat on or off the trailer. One tip is to rub the top of the carpeted bunks with a block of paraffin wax.

Rollers let the boat easily glide on and off the trailer, which comes in especially handy if you're launching the boat by yourself. If you don't have enough of the trailer in the water, however, the boat may fall off the trailer before it's completely in the water. Another downside to rollers is that, over a period of time, they can leave small indentations in the bottom of the boat.

So which system is best? It depends on the size of your boat and on where and how often you use it. For powerboats up to 25 feet long that are launched from well-designed and maintained ramps, a bunk trailer will be fine. But if your boat is heavier than 2,500 pounds or longer than 25 feet, or if you have a very small boat that you can safely launch from the roadside directly into the water without a ramp, I recommend using rollers to make things easier.

Axle and wheels

Under the bunks or rollers are the *axle* and *wheels*. Small boats (up to 20 feet) can get by with a single-axle trailer, whereas larger, heavier boats require more axles to support the weight. Single-axle trailers are lighter and easier to tow, and they will go around corners easier than trailers with dual axles.

Heavier boats require a dual-axle trailer, which normally has *surge brakes* that manually apply whenever the tow vehicle suddenly slows. For heavier boats, some trailers have *electric brakes*, which are wired to the braking system of the tow vehicle and engage whenever the vehicle brakes are applied. Because the wheels on dual-axle trailers always point forward, going straight is easy, but turning tight corners is more difficult. It's normal for the trailer to "hop" through a turn because the tires are scrubbing sideways, but going slow for tight maneuvering helps.

Greasable fittings are designed to let you lubricate the trailer bearings without having to disassemble the wheels.

Some trailers come with wheels and tires that are much smaller than the tow vehicle's tires, which means the trailer rides closer to the ground and is more stable. However, small tires (with a diameter of 12 inches or less) get hotter faster, wear out more quickly, and don't provide as much cushioning for the boat as larger tires do. If you trailer your boat fewer than 25 miles each way and the boat is less than 20 feet long and 1,500 pounds, small tires will do fine. Larger tires (with a diameter of 13 inches or greater) provide more ground clearance, support more weight, and rotate more slowly, making them ideal for heavier boats (greater than 2,000 pounds) and longer towing distances (30 miles or more).

Trailering your boat allows you to expand your boating adventures by taking the boat to explore new waters.

Be sure to have a spare tire, a good lug-nut wrench, and a jack that works on the trailer. The best way to make sure nothing breaks or goes wrong is to perform regular maintenance, paying attention to the condition of your trailer and its parts—if it looks worn out, it probably is and should be replaced immediately. Also, many small boat trailers aren't equipped with brakes because those on the tow vehicle are sufficient, but to be safe, it's also a good idea to have at least a set of surge brakes installed. It's also a good idea to check your state requirements because several states require brakes on all trailers, no matter how light duty they may be.

Transom tie-down

While it's not technically part of the trailer, the *transom tie-down* strap is as important as any of the main components, because it holds the boat on the trailer. Tie-downs come in two styles: a *gunwale strap* or a *transom strap*. Gunwale straps lie across the boat and are padded where they come into contact with the sides of the boat. Transom straps run from the two eyebolts on the outside of the transom straight down to the trailer. They are simple to use but, because they may not hold the boat as securely as a gunwale strap, should be used only on small boats (17 feet and under).

Safety chains

The two chains at the front of the trailer are called the *safety chains* and are designed to keep the trailer attached to the tow

A WORD OF CAUTION

• • • • • • • • • • • • • • • • • • •

Backing the tow vehicle to the trailer seems simple enough, but the first time you try it (and every time thereafter) you'll find out how good your communication skills actually are. It helps to have another person stand off to the side where she can see the trailer and your tow hitch ball. Because it can be difficult for you to gauge distance as you drive, this person can direct you as you back toward the trailer.

Mastering this technique requires practice and patience, but here's a helpful trick: after you have connected the trailer to the tow vehicle, *immediately* place one strip of brightly colored tape on the back of the winch and another on the back window of your tow vehicle. When you are seated in the driver's seat, you will be able to look back to see that the two strips of tape are perfectly aligned. With this tape in place, the next time you want to connect the trailer to the tow vehicle, all you will need to do is line up the two pieces of tape. You'll be ready to go without having to yell back and forth to a helper.

Carrying a **spare drain plug** on your boat keychain can save the day if the first plug is lost or misplaced.

vehicle in case the coupler comes loose from the tow hitch ball. This hardly ever happens, but if it does, you'll be glad you have safety chains.

Tongue jack

Your trailer may also have a stationary or folding *tongue jack*, which is used to hold the trailer level when it isn't attached to the tow vehicle. Tongue jacks are useful because they let you store the boat level, which makes it easier to work on the boat while it's on the trailer and also prevents water from accumulating at either end. When storing the boat, adjust the tongue jack to keep the boat tilted slightly upward, so that any water that gets in will quickly run out through the drain holes at the transom.

HITTING THE ROAD

Towing a boat when you're driving in a straight line is easy, but when you throw in a few curves or need to back the boat up, things start getting complicated. The most important thing to do is *pay attention* the entire time you are trailering. Any vehicle handles differently when connected to a trailer: it accelerates more slowly, makes wider turns, takes longer to stop, and is harder to park.

If a traffic light ahead turns yellow, start braking well in advance. Drive as if you need three times as much space to stop, keeping ample space between you and any vehicles in front of you. Having a loaded trailer behind you is like having a hand push you forward, and there's nothing worse than helplessly sliding through a red light with your brakes locked. If you trailer long enough, this will happen (it's most common on rainy afternoons). For this reason, you should

"**I** clearly remember hitting the same bump in the road I always did when I was about two blocks away from home, but this time when I checked my rearview mirror, my boat's trailer had come loose from the hitch ball and was bouncing along behind me, connected only by the safety chains. I'd always wondered if they could hold the boat and trailer, and now I knew for sure."

—Pam Richter, Boston, Massachusetts

TRAILERING CHECKLIST

Before heading down the road with your boat on the trailer, always take the following steps.

- Fasten all containers, hatches, and lids on the boat.
- Store any loose objects on the boat in onboard cabinets or bins.
- Make sure the stern-drive or outboard engine is tilted in the raised position to avoid hitting the road.
- Store all loose cushions, PFDs, and fenders.
- Check the trailer tires for proper inflation. If the tires appear to have an excessive bulge, they may be underinflated.
- Check the trailer tires for cracks on the sidewalls that could cause a blowout while on the road.
- Use a lug-nut wrench once per month to make sure the trailer lug nuts stay tight.
- Lower antennas and flag stanchions, and remove any fishing rods from rod holders.
- Make sure all trailer tie-downs are securely fastened on the boat as well as on the trailer.
- Check all trailer rollers for cracks and to make sure the rollers still roll.
- Inspect the trailer wiring harness for bare or broken wires. Make sure all of the bulbs function, and replace them as necessary.
- Inspect the winch cable for frays and corrosion.
- Make sure the removable winch handle is packed in the tow vehicle where it can easily be found.
- Inspect the ball hitch to make sure it is tightly fastened.
- Lower the boat's folding top prior to trailering the boat over the highway.
- Inspect the trailer safety chains for cracks and corrosion.
- Tighten the bolts holding the trailer license plate in place.
- Replace (or remove) the boat's drain plugs.
- Check that the boat's battery switch is in the "off" position.

practice towing the trailer—preferably in a large, empty parking lot—just as if you were learning to drive a car.

You'll need to take turns a lot wider because the trailer can't turn as tightly as the tow vehicle. Use your mirrors to keep an eye on the trailer, watching that it doesn't ride up on curbs. (If your tow vehicle's mirrors aren't large enough to let you see all the way to the back of the trailer, your local truck rental dealer can help you install bigger ones, or you can purchase strap-on mirrors for easy removal when you're not trailering.) Trailers follow the path of the tow vehicle best when going straight or making left-hand turns, but you'll need a lot more room when turning right. You may need to cut into the left-hand lane, so plan your turns for when there are no vehicles or pedestrians in your path.

Avoid detours and side trips. Even if you're trailering a small boat, when it's on a trailer it can double the length of your tow vehicle, making any convenience stops difficult. If you need to get gas,

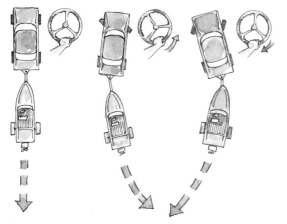

When **backing up** the trailer, if your hands are on the **bottom** of the steering wheel (6 o'clock), turn your tow vehicle's steering wheel in the **same** direction you want the trailer to go (shown); if you keep your hands at the *top* of the wheel (12 o'clock), turn in the direction *opposite* to where you want the trailer to go (not shown).

carefully choose a gas station that has high overheads, and use the pump closest to the road, approaching so that the boat is between the pump and the road.

On multilane roads, stay in the right-hand lane as much as possible. If you need to pass another vehicle, use your turn signals and start to pass only when there is no oncoming traffic. It will take longer to pass than you expect, but once clear, don't just swing back in—keep going until you can clearly see the other vehicle in your rearview mirrors.

BACKING UP

At some point, you *will* have to back up, whether it's to launch or retrieve the boat or to park the trailer. Backing up is daunting at first, because the trailer will seem to have a mind of its own. But, believe it or not, backing is actually one of the easiest things to do, once you've learned the following secrets.

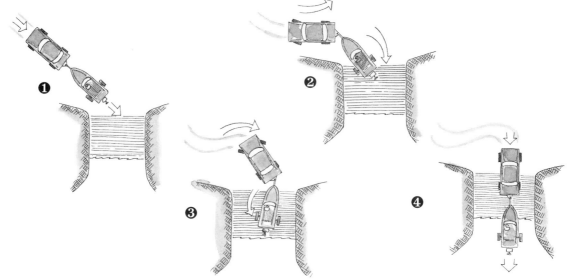

Negotiating a trailer in reverse. **1.** When driving in reverse, remember that the car and trailer move in opposite left-right directions. **2.** Cut the car in so that the front of the trailer moves out. **3.** Change the direction of the car wheels (the front of the trailer will move back in) and back slowly down the ramp as the trailer moves to the right. **4.** When the trailer is centered on the ramp, straighten the car wheels to follow the trailer straight down the ramp.

First, have your passengers leave the car and wait in a shady place. Next, sit with your left hand on the base of the steering wheel and face backward, looking through the back window or over your left shoulder out the side window. When you want to turn the trailer to the left, pull your hand to the left—*making sure you keep facing backward* (switch the motion to turn in the opposite direction). Keep in mind that the trailer will move in the opposite direction of the car. Go slow, and if you need to start over, just pull forward until the trailer straightens out behind you and begin again. It's normal for the trailer to wander a bit from side to side, so make whatever opposite correc-

Once you're used to the routine, it'll take you less than 15 minutes to get your boat from ramp to water.

tions are needed to keep it backing in a mostly straight line. With a little practice, you'll be able to back the trailer without much back-and-forthing.

LAUNCHING FROM THE TRAILER

OK, you've made it to the ramp and the boat is ready to back down to the water. You've made sure the drain plug is in the boat, the gunwale tie-down has been removed and stored in the tow vehicle, the pigtail for the trailer lights is disconnected, there's plenty of room at the dock for you to tie up the boat when it floats off the trailer, the motor is tilted in the "up" position so it won't dig into the ramp surface, and your crew is standing alongside the dock holding the bow and stern lines, which are running under the bow and side rails.

Slowly back the trailer down the ramp toward the water, making sure you're lining up alongside the dock (about a foot away is close enough). Carefully back the trailer toward and into the water to the point it begins to float but not so far that your tow vehicle's rear tires get wet—it's important that the rear tires have traction for driving back up the ramp. When the trailer is halfway submerged—or as soon as the boat begins to float—stop, set your vehicle's parking brake, and have your crew hold on to the bow and stern lines, which should be about twice the length of the boat to allow your crew to walk next to the boat as you back it into the water. To prevent injury, your crew should have no more than a light grip on the lines.

With the boat just barely floating above the partially submerged trailer, you can now use the winch to let the boat slide into the water and float free, with your crew ready on the dock-lines to pull it snug to the dock and secure it. Once the boat is securely tied, unsnap the bow cable from the boat and winch the loose end back in. After making sure the boat is floating,

bow eye

Trailer bow straps should be inspected for wear every time you connect them to the boat when winching it out of the water and back onto the trailer.

carefully drive forward in order to pull the trailer out from under the boat. Drive back up the ramp and park.

RETRIEVING THE BOAT

After a day on the water, it's time to retrieve the boat. With the boat tied securely to the dock out of the way, engine off and the lower unit tilted up, back the trailer into the water until the rear portion of the bunks or rollers is submerged, and set the tow vehicle's parking brake. Boat ramps are more slippery than you would expect, so if you need to walk down one, *be careful*. Use the bow and stern lines to lead the boat to the trailer, and guide the bow between the bunks or rollers.

When the boat is floating with its bow over the trailer bunks or rollers, reverse the winch gear and pull out enough cable to reach the bow eye. Attach the cable, flick the gear switch to the "retrieve" position, and then begin cranking the winch handle. Watch how the cable is taken up on the spool to make sure it stays neatly wrapped and doesn't wander from side to side where it can suddenly come loose. Keep cranking the winch so that the boat fits snugly into the rubber V extending from the winch. Attach the trailer's bow strap to the boat's U-bolt.

You may see other powerboaters drive the boat onto the trailer and then use the engine to force the boat up onto the trailer; if you are new to boating, this is a great way to launch the boat right on top of the tow vehicle. Instead, do it right, take it slow, and if the boat starts going sideways, it's OK to push it back and start over again. Keep in mind that a cable under tension can snap and injure bystanders, so don't let anyone stand next to the cable while you're pulling the boat onto the trailer.

When the boat's bow is snugged up into the V on the trailer winch, the bow strap is in place, and the transom tie-downs are secured, you're done. Slowly drive up the ramp, stop when you're clear of it, and give the winch a few more cranks to take up any slack that might occur once the boat is level. Now reattach the gunwale tie-down, open the drain plug to let any accumulated water flow out, reconnect the trailer lights, pack up your crew, and go home (see the sidebar on page 91 for a full prejourney checklist). Once home, you'll need to flush the engine (see page 120), rinse the hull, clean up any messes, and put the gear away. Congratulations! You're now a trailering powerboater!

Chapter 8

SAFETY AND COMFORT

Powerboating can seem daunting if you're new to it; as you pull away from the dock, you and your passengers are on your own, and as the boatowner, you're responsible for making sure they have a good time and return safely. But unlike driving a car, if the boat has a mechanical problem, or someone becomes ill, you can't just pull over to the side. The trick is to be prepared for most situations, even if that just means knowing when to call for help.

With proper maintenance, a powerboat can be expected to provide many years of reliable service, and by practicing a few simple safety precautions like having your passengers wear PFDs and sunblock, you can forestall many potential problems. When practiced with common sense, boating is a thoroughly enjoyable and very safe activity—it does require a high degree of diligence from you as the boatowner or -operator, but that comes with a feeling of self-confidence that grows with every successful adventure on the water.

STAYING IN TOUCH

One of the best things about time spent on the water is being away from the things that contribute to stress, including phones. But there are times when you don't want to be completely cut off from the rest of the world, especially in the case of an emergency. For this reason, many powerboaters equip their craft with *cellular phones* or *VHF (very high frequency) radios*—or both.

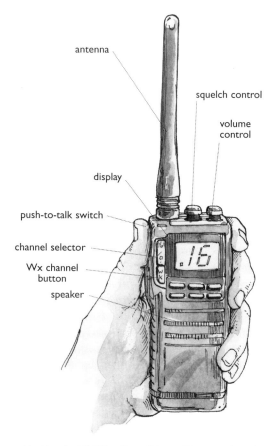

antenna

squelch control

volume control

display

push-to-talk switch

channel selector

Wx channel button

speaker

Most **handheld VHF radios** will have either a touch pad or knobs to control the functions for volume, squelch, channel selections, weather channel, instant channel-16 access, and power settings.

You should at least equip your boat with a VHF radiotelephone, which can be a fixed-mount or handheld portable unit and allows boaters to both monitor weather channels and communicate with one another, the coast guard, drawbridge operators, public telephone operators, and marinas. Unless you carry passengers for hire, you don't need a license to operate a VHF radio on your boat.

A typical VHF can access up to 90 channels, but the channels you'll use most are channel 16 to report an emergency, channel 9 to make initial contact with other boats, channel 13 to call bridge tenders, and usually channels 68, 69, 71, or 72 to speak to other boats or marinas. Channel 24 is reserved for the public telephone marine operator so you can use the VHF to make regular telephone calls. The range of a VHF radio is related to the height of its antenna—a handheld VHF with its short antenna can transmit to others up to a few miles away, whereas a fixed-mount VHF radio with a 6- or 8-foot antenna can transmit and receive signals over much longer distances.

If you do have a VHF on board, the law requires that you have it set to channel 16 so you can be aware of any other boats in your area that may need emergency assistance. The U.S. Coast Guard and local marine enforcement agencies constantly monitor channel 16, so you can always get help if you need it. You can also use channel 16 to initiate contact, or *hail*, another boat or a marina, but it's better to use channel 9 and save channel 16 for emergency calls. When you do hail another boat, immediately switch to a working channel like 68 or 69 for your conversation so other boats can then use channel 9. If you want information about the weather, switch to one of the weather (Wx) channels to hear the latest forecast for your area. Even though you can contact the marine operator to make a telephone call using your VHF, it isn't a substitute for a telephone. In some areas that are out of the range of cellular telephones, however, your VHF may be your only link to the rest of the world.

There are no monthly or per-minute costs for using a VHF radio, and with handheld units available for as little as $100, these radios are cheap insurance and a good way to stay in touch. Keep in mind, though, that anyone in the area with a VHF radio can hear your conversation. Also, don't use it anywhere other than on your powerboat; it's illegal to use a VHF radio on land.

HOW DO I USE A VHF RADIO?

VHF radios are handy to have, even if all you do is listen to the weather forecast and monitor channel 16. But what happens when you want to reach out and touch someone? Let's say you are on your powerboat (named *Hers*, of course) and are trying to contact friends on another boat named *Freestyle*. First, adjust the volume knob to a comfortable level. Next, turn the "squelch" knob until you hear static, then turn it back just enough to cut off the static, and the radio is ready to use. To talk on the radio, press the button on the side of the microphone. Start on channel 16 and hail the other boat like this: "*Freestyle, Freestyle, Freestyle,* this is *Hers.*" If the other boat hears you, they will respond right away, saying something like "*Hers,* this is *Freestyle.* Switch to 68." By changing channels to 68, you free up channel 16 for emergency calls.

If the boat you're calling doesn't respond, wait at least five minutes before calling them again. An even better way is to make plans beforehand to contact each other at a certain time on channel 68. Remember that only one person at a time can transmit on a given radio channel. To avoid confusion say "over" to indicate you've released the microphone button so the other party can respond.

If you have an emergency and need to call for help, the internationally recognized term for an emergency at sea is *Mayday.* When you hear this term, you'll be amazed at the response the call gets. It should be used only in a life-threatening emergency, not to announce you have run out of gas, run aground, or can't start the engine (use channel 16 to call a marine assistance firm, which will send a towboat to assist you). The idea of a Mayday call is to let the world know who you are, what the problem is, and your location; in a severe emergency, there may not be time to talk with rescuers. (See the sidebar at right for an example of a Mayday transmission.) Weems and Plath makes a self-adhesive "script card" that you can place next to your VHF radio; this card will walk anyone—even a novice VHF user—through the entire Mayday call procedure.

REQUIRED SAFETY AND EMERGENCY EQUIPMENT

Every time any boat—powered or unpowered—leaves the dock for any length of time, it must have on board a specific collection

USING A VHF RADIO TO CALL FOR HELP

● ● ● ● ● ● ● ● ● ● ● ● ● ● ● ● ● ● ● ●

"**Mayday, Mayday, Mayday, this is** *Hers, Hers, Hers.* **My position is** [*if you have a GPS, read the coordinates on it, or if you can see landmarks, describe them*]. **Our situation is** [*describe the emergency—a fire, a passenger has been lost overboard, you hit a submerged log and are taking on water, or whatever else may have happened*]. **We need assistance** [*if you need medical help, say so; if you need pumps to stay afloat; say that as well*]. **There are** [*give correct number*] **persons aboard, and we have the following safety equipment** [*describe what safety gear is aboard, such as PFDs, flares, or first-aid kits*]. **My boat is** [*describe the boat as precisely as you can, for example, "a white 32-foot express cruiser with a red Bimini top and a red hull stripe"*]. **I will be monitoring channel 16. This is** *Hers,* **over."**

Some **inflatable PFDs**, such as this fanny-pack style, are so comfortable that you might forget to take them off.

of safety equipment. If a coast guard or local law enforcement boat stops you for a routine safety inspection, you can be fined if your boat isn't properly equipped. The list of required equipment includes the following items.

Personal flotation devices (PFDs)

Sometimes called *life jackets*, PFDs are designed to keep a person afloat. They are divided into five inherently buoyant types (1 through 5), which differ in how much buoyancy they provide, what they look like, whether they'll float you faceup, and where they are meant to be used. The coast guard allows recreational boaters who don't go more than 25 miles from shore to choose the type of PFD they use; most boaters opt for the Type 2 and 3 models, which we'll look at below.

The Type 1 PFD, an *offshore life jacket*, provides the most flotation of any PFD and is approved for use on any waters (including the open ocean) because it will float an unconscious wearer faceup for extended periods of time. The Type 2 PFD, a *near-shore life vest*, is intended for use on calm waters, such as on lakes or close to shore. A Type 2 will hold the wearer faceup, but because it is a bib-style design, it won't always automatically turn an unconscious person faceup.

Type 3 PFDs are *flotation aids*. Less bulky than Type 1 or Type 2 PFDs, this type includes PFDs designed to look like windbreakers or vests. This type provides the same buoyancy as a Type 2 model, but it won't float an unconscious person faceup. In addition to the windbreaker style, Stearns and Sporting Lives make Type 3 inflatable vests that look like suspenders, which either can be manually activated or will automatically inflate when they get wet.

A Type 4 PFD is a *throwable device*. This type includes the round, orange ring buoys and the yellow horseshoe-shaped life rings you see on the rails of commercial passenger boats and at the lifeguard station at a pool. The idea is to throw them to a person in the water to hang onto until help can get to them. These PFDs also come in square shapes that double as extra seat cushions.

• •

"**I**f you think wearing a PFD is uncomfortable, trying treading water for thirty minutes without one. Last summer, I was swimming next to the boat when the current swept me away, and it took half an hour for them to reach me. When we got back to the dock, I went straight to the store and bought a Type 3 vest that fits me perfectly, and I wear it every time I'm on the boat."

—Nora Whitfield, Sacramento, California

• •

Although designed to be worn in an emergency, an inherently buoyant PFD such as these **Type 2** (left) and **Type 3** (right) **vests** can be thrown, with a line attached, to a person in the water.

A Type 5 PFD is a *special-use device*. This type can be either the model found under the seats of commercial airliners (which is slipped over the head and inflated by pulling on a cord) or the model designed to resemble a windbreaker jacket with a built-in inflatable vest.

For many recreational powerboaters, a Type 3 windbreaker or vest-style PFD is all you need, and is what you or your passengers are most likely to wear. No matter how good a swimmer you are—and especially so if you aren't a good swimmer—you'll be a lot safer just by slipping it on. When choosing PFDs, look for the "USCG-Approved" label, and try your choice on to make sure it fits. If you're a small woman, you may only fit in a child's PFD, but because it might not have enough flotation to keep your head above water, try it in the water before you actually rely on it. Many department stores carry PFDs, but you'll find the best selection of styles and sizes by shopping at a marine supply store like West Marine or BoatU.S.; if there isn't a store in your area, you can call and ask either company to send you one of their comprehensive catalogs (see the resources chapter for contact information).

Fire extinguisher

Fire extinguishers are rated according to the type of fires they can put out. The easiest way to make sure a fire extinguisher is designed for marine use is to look for a "USCG-Approved" label on the casing. In order to be legal, almost all powerboats up to 26 feet long need to have at least one USCG-approved type B-1 extinguisher on board; larger powerboats are required to have additional fire extinguishers. Although a few powerboats, such as those with open deck layouts, are not legally required to carry a fire extinguisher, it's still a good idea to have a fire extinguisher on hand.

A fire on board can spread more quickly than you can imagine, so it's vitally important to attempt to put out the fire as soon as possible. Store your fire extinguisher where it is readily accessible, such as within reach of the helm or in the galley by the stove. To use a fire extinguisher properly, remove the safety pin from the lever, aim the nozzle at the base of the fire, press the lever to activate the extinguisher, and use a sweeping motion to smother the flames. Have everyone

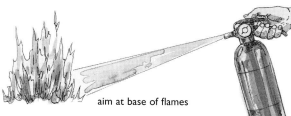

aim at base of flames

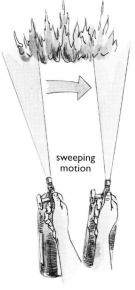

sweeping motion

The fastest and most effective way to douse a fire is to aim the extinguisher at the base of the flames, activate the trigger, and use a sweeping motion to smother the flames.

move as far away from the fire as possible (including jumping off the boat if necessary and swimming away from any burning fuel on the surface).

If possible, while you're working on putting out the fire and keeping the passengers a safe distance from the flames, ask one of your passengers to call 911 on a cellular phone or use VHF channel 16 to alert the coast guard to the situation. Because grease fires in the galley are the second most likely type of onboard fire (behind engine fires), keep an open box of baking soda or a chemically treated *fire towel* nearby; either will quickly smother a small fire when tossed over the flames.

Some larger powerboats with enclosed engine compartments may have built-in fire extinguishing systems that use a smothering gas like Halon or carbon dioxide. These systems are usually activated either automatically or by means of a switch located away from the engine compartment; if your powerboat has such a remote switch, make sure you know where it is. Because some of the gases used to extinguish fire can be lethal, be very careful opening the engine compartment after activating the system.

Sound-producing devices

This category includes such devices as whistles, bells, and portable air horns; they are intended to make sure other boats in the area are aware of your presence. If you find yourself on the water during a heavy rainstorm or fog, you may not be able to see other boats; or, if your boat is

"**W**e were cruising down the Mississippi late one night, and as we went around every curve, we'd honk an air horn to let oncoming boats know we were there. We'd then hear the horn of any approaching boats, but at one curve there was no response. Just as we rounded the curve, a huge barge came rushing at us, and we barely missed being hit by it. The tug pushing the barge hadn't heard our signal and had no idea we were in front of him. He apologized, but we started rounding corners a whole lot more carefully after that."

—Leigh Taylor, Natchez, Mississippi

small, it may not be easily visible to larger boats. Using a sound signal enables other boats to hear you and thus know you are nearby. Sound signals can also be used in clear weather, such as when you're approaching a blind curve in a channel or river, or when you're entering a busy waterway from a narrow channel. Use your whistle or horn to make a single prolonged blast for about four seconds; if there are any boats coming from the other direction, they'll know to look out for you (they're also supposed to respond with their horn to let you know they heard you).

Navigation lights

These are the red, green, and white lights found on all powerboats to make it easier to avoid collisions. By understanding the locations of these lights, you can tell which direction another boat is traveling and can stay out of its way simply by seeing only its lights in the dark (see chapter 5 for a complete description of each light's location and meaning). Turn your navigation lights on before it gets dark, or when you run into a rainstorm, fog, or anything else that could hamper your own visibility or another boater's ability to see you.

Visual distress signals

These include signal flares, smoke flares, strobe lights, a flashlight, or anything else that will attract attention from a distance in daylight or at night. The coast guard requires all boats longer than 16 feet to carry night and day signals and boats shorter than 16 feet to carry night signals, even if the boats aren't usually used after dark.

A *day signal* is a form of attention-getting device that can be seen in normal daylight conditions, including *pyrotechnic flares*, a *smoke flare*, or a brightly colored flag. Smoke flares (cans of smoke) are for daylight use only. Be sure to open them so the smoke will blow away from your powerboat, instead of over or across it. A *night signal* is a device that can be seen easily in dark or low-light conditions. Examples of night signals include *electronic strobes* (which can also be used during the day, but not as effectively) and pyrotechnic flares.

The most common type of signals used by powerboaters are pyrotechnic flares—particularly *meteor flares*, which are packaged in groups of three and are launched from either a *flare gun* or a *handheld launcher*. Visual distress signals are meant to be used only in an emergency (not on the Fourth of July!) and need to be handled carefully because they can easily cause injuries or damage.

"**A**fter boating for 15 years, I'd never used any of my emergency equipment. When I took a coworker for her first powerboat cruise, the engine conked out and what was supposed to be a hour-long cruise turned into an after-dark adventure. I didn't have a VHF radio then, so I used my flare gun to attract the attention of a boat that passed by several hours later, and we got a tow back to the dock."

—Mary Turner, New Orleans, Louisiana

Signal flares, smoke flares, and meteor flares are stamped with expiration dates (42 months after manufacture), and in order to meet coast guard requirements, you must have at least three nonexpired flares on your boat. Expired flares usually will still work, however, so it's a good idea to keep them as spares in case of emergency.

FUEL SAFETY

Powerboating is one of the safer sports you can pursue, but because it involves machinery and engines, it requires a higher level of attention than if you were playing golf or tennis, for example. As with a car, you start a powerboat with the ignition key, but there are some important differences, especially for those with inboard gasoline engines. We all have fantasies of jumping aboard a sleek raceboat, starting the engines, and roaring out of the harbor, but there are a few good reasons why this is best left a fantasy.

Gasoline fumes are extremely flammable. Because they are heavier than air, they can "sink" to the bottom of an enclosed engine compartment, or into the area under the floor of the boat, called the *bilge*, where they could be ignited by a spark when an engine is started. Because any gasoline engine can produce explosive fumes, it's important to make sure any powerboat with an inboard gas engine is equipped with a *bilge blower*, a fan that circulates air out of the enclosed engine compartment. Before turning the ignition key, the bilge blower should run for at least five minutes; this wait may seem tedious, but a boat is most likely to catch fire while it's being started.

Because outboard engines are mounted "outside" the boat, they don't need blowers and can be started right away. While outboard engines are almost always gasoline powered, inboard engines run on either gasoline or diesel fuel. Diesel fumes aren't explosive. You can easily tell a diesel from a gas engine because diesel engines don't have spark plugs.

Also use caution while you're filling the powerboat's fuel tanks. Whether the boat is on a trailer behind your car at a gas station or tied to a waterfront fuel dock, as gasoline is pumped into the

Top: A **strobe light** should be attached to all PFDs when the boat is operated at night, during stormy weather, or in high seas. **Bottom:** When firing **flares**, always aim the flare gun or launcher up and downwind of the boat to prevent a burning flare from drifting back onto the boat.

Above: Found along most popular waterways, **fuel docks** often offer the amenities of a convenience store, including rest rooms. **Right:** Refueling at a marina fuel dock often is the most convenient option.

tank, explosive fumes are pushed out. Turn off the engine, have all the passengers leave the boat, and shut off any electric fans or anything else that could create a spark (including putting out cigarettes). If your powerboat has a galley, make sure the stove is not on. Close all ports and hatches to keep fumes from entering closed areas of the boat, and make sure a fire extinguisher is within easy reach.

Keep an eye on the fuel pump, too; by knowing the capacity of your fuel tank (it may be stamped or painted onto the side of the tank; if not, call the manufacturer), you can estimate how many gallons you need to add. If you add too much fuel into the tank, some of it can spill out the vent and into the water or onto the ground, causing environmental damage. The U.S. Coast Guard takes all fuel spills very seriously and can fine you even for a small one. Once the fuel tank is full, wipe up any spills with an absorbent cloth, securely close the tank fill cap, and dispose of the cloth in a proper trash container. Run the blower fan for at least five minutes after fueling, and then sniff the bilge area to check for gas fumes before you start the engines or let passengers back onto the boat.

If you're taking your boat on a long cruise and are concerned about having enough fuel or being able to find a fuel dock, you may want to carry spare fuel aboard. If you do, use only Department of Transportation–approved fuel containers (available at marine supply stores or hardware stores), and store them in well-ventilated areas, well away from the cabin, the galley, or any sources of sparks or flame.

If your powerboat has a removable fuel tank that you refill at a gasoline station, always place the tank completely on the ground before you open the cap and add gas; static electricity is formed when gas is pumped into the tank and could ignite the gas vapors, causing damage and possibly serious injuries. Outboard motors are designed to use "regular" unleaded gasoline, which is usually less expensive. If you have a two-stroke outboard (see page 120), you will need to add oil to the gas before using it. If you trailer your powerboat, you can refuel either at a gas station or at a waterfront fuel dock; fuel is normally less expensive at the gas station, but sometimes it's worth it to pay more for the convenience of refueling at a fuel dock. Even if you have a lot of trailering experience, maneuvering a car and trailer around gas pumps can be more adventure than you want, especially if you have to aim for the middle aisle to reach an empty pump.

WHAT TO DO IF SOMETHING GOES WRONG

Most modern powerboats are fairly simple. There's really not a lot to do in order to keep your powerboat's engine running smoothly except for checking the oil and gas levels. (See chapter 9 for information about basic maintenance.) If something does happen that causes the engine to malfunction, however, the first thing to do is make sure the passengers and the boat are safe—in that order. Once you know your passengers are OK, it's time to secure the boat. If the problem happens at a dock and you're still tied alongside, stay where you are. On the other hand, if you're under way when the engine conks out, first try restarting the engine. It isn't common, but sometimes a bit of dirt will clog the fuel filter, causing a temporary shutdown that cures itself as soon as the engine stalls.

If you can't restart the engine, try to get the attention of passing boaters who can give you a tow to the closest dock. If you can't get a tow this way, you can use your VHF radio to call a marine assistance company like Sea Tow. Professional marine towing firms have the equipment and expertise to get your boat to a safe place, and several offer annual memberships that provide free towing and assistance services in case you run out of fuel or run aground.

CREW OVERBOARD AND WHAT TO DO

One of the worst things that can happen during a cruise is to have one of your passengers fall over the side. If this happens, first of all do not panic. If there are other people on the boat, immediately instruct one of them to act as spotter, keeping an eye on and pointing at the person in the water until she's back in the boat. By having a dedicated spotter, you can focus on driving the boat while referring to where they are pointing as a reference point.

With luck, the person in the water will be wearing her PFD, which will keep her afloat and easier to locate. If, because of bad weather, high seas, or any other reason, you are unable to locate the person in the water, immediately use channel 16 of your VHF radio to notify the coast guard of the situation. By doing so, you will be mobilizing as many people and other boats to find the person as soon as possible. The best thing you can do is remain calm and continue looking for the person

HELPING OTHER BOATERS IN NEED OF A TOW

Sooner or later, when you're out on the water you will come across another boater who for one reason or another needs a tow. The boat might have run out of fuel, it might have a drained battery that can't start the engine, or it might have run aground in a shallow area.

Although it seems harsh, sometimes the best way you can help a stranded boater is to offer to use your cellular phone or VHF radio to call a marine assistance towing company. There's a lot more to towing a boat than just tossing a line to the other boat and hauling it to the nearest dock. Because boats are heavy, an inordinate amount of strain is placed on the tow line. If it isn't secured properly, it could rip off a cleat on either boat, or it could come loose during the tow, which could cause problems if, for example, it happened in the middle of a busy channel. If the strain causes the line to break, the line can come hurtling back with enough speed and force to damage to the boat or to seriously injure a passenger.

If the other boat is aground, you run the risk of also being grounded by approaching it. And even if the other boat is smaller than your boat, if the grounded boat is stuck in soft sand or mud, it may take more force than your boat's engine can provide to break the boat free, or the strain on your cleats could loosen them so they become projectiles. If the other boat was damaged when it grounded, it could begin to take on water when pulled free, causing a whole new set of problems. Yet another reason to call a professional is that most boats carry only relatively short lengths of dockline, which are not well suited for towing other boats.

Restricted visibility because of weather or darkness is a condition under which you should never attempt to tow another boat before seeking assistance from a marine towing company.

No matter how well intentioned you may be, by trying to tow someone with your boat you could end up damaging your boat or the other boat—or, worse still, someone could get hurt in the process.

That being said, if you decide to provide a tow, here are the basics:

Using the strongest line available (double-braided nylon line is best, three-strand twisted nylon is the worst), secure it on your boat only to through-bolted cleats or U-bolts at or near the transom—if the cleat is attached using wood screws, do not attempt a tow because of the possibility of damaging your boat and perhaps injuring someone. If the other boat is grounded, attach the loose end of the tow line to a floating fender or PFD and float it to them to avoid bringing your boat too close to danger.

Have the towed boat attach their end of their line to the strongest cleat or U-bolt available at the bow. To prevent injuries if the tow line breaks, have everyone on the towed boat put on PFDs and stay low and well away from the tow line and attachment point. As an extra precaution, have the skipper of the other boat stay prepared to cut the tow line in case of an emergency.

When you are ready to tow the other boat, apply throttle gradually and smoothly—your boat wasn't designed to be a tugboat, so go slow and easy. Have a passenger on either boat stand by with an air horn in case you need to alert approaching boats that you have a vessel in tow—use the horns as you go around any blind turns or pass an intersecting waterway (one prolonged blast followed by two short blasts).

● ●

"**W**e were on our way back to the dock from a day of scuba diving when we ran aground one night at low tide in the middle of Biscayne Bay. No one responded to our radio calls, and we had to wait until the tide came up enough to float free. Since no one knew we were overdue, nobody was looking for us. We made it back OK, but I learned a lesson."

—Lori Jacobs, Pembroke Pines, Florida

● ●

until she is found and back in the boat, at which time you'll need to determine whether she requires first aid or medical attention.

You should also use channel 16 to notify the coast guard and other boaters in the immediate area if a person has fallen overboard in an area with a lot of other boat traffic. By alerting other boaters of a person overboard, they can assist in the search for the person as well as proceed carefully in order to avoid hitting her.

Some powerboaters use an electronic crew-overboard alarm, which alerts you immediately if anyone falls overboard. This alarm consists of a transmitter that is attached to a PFD and an alarm located on the boat; when the transmitter gets wet, it sounds the alarm.

EPIRBS AND WHEN TO USE THEM

Emergency position-indicating radio beacons (EPIRBs) transmit a radio signal that allows rescue agencies to home in on their position. Because an EPIRB is the easiest and most foolproof way of letting someone know you need help, I always carry one on my boat. With the simple flipping of a switch, the EPIRB automatically transmits a signal, a faster alternative to VHF radios or cellular phones when there isn't time to call for help. Some EPIRBs will automatically begin to transmit a signal as soon as they are submerged.

There are two types of EPIRBs, which differ in the type of signal they transmit and in price. For about $200, you can get a Class B EPIRB, such as the ACR Mini B2, that transmits a 121.5 MHz radio signal received by aircraft. A Class B signal gives rescuers a 12-square-mile area to look for you. Class A EPIRBs use a 406 MHz signal that is received by and relayed via satellite, so it will work anywhere in the world. Class A models, such as the ACR RapidFix, cost about $800, but they're a lot more precise, giving rescuers a 2-square-mile search area. In addition, Class A units are registered to each owner, so they also transmit information on who you are and what type of boat you have, letting rescuers know not only where to look but also who they're looking for. Some of the newer Class A EPIRBs can also be connected to a GPS unit, providing rescuers with your exact location and eliminating the need for a search.

FLOAT PLANS AND HOW TO FILE THEM

Even if you plan only a simple day of casual cruising on your powerboat, you normally have a rough idea of when you plan to leave the dock, where you might go, and what time you expect

COB DRILL

● ●

Everyone aboard your boat should know where the PFDs and first-aid kit are—and what to do in the event of someone falling overboard.

Before running the COB (crew overboard) drill, make sure everyone aboard is wearing a properly sized PFD, and the boat is clear of other boat traffic in calm waters. Designate a flotable cushion as the COB (crew overboard) and chuck it overboard while running at speed. Immediately yell "Crew overboard," and appoint one person to do nothing but locate and point at the COB, yelling "Crew overboard port!" or "Crew overboard starboard!" as appropriate. Checking for other boat traffic, turn the boat around to come back to the COB—with your pointer-yeller showing its location, you're free to watch for other boat traffic. Slow the boat as you approach the COB, and turn off the engine when you're about 15 feet away so you can drift alongside it—never approach anyone in the water with the engine on or with the propeller turning. Haul the cushion aboard.

Let your passengers ask questions so they're clear on what to do if the situation had been real. Where is the line, with a PFD attached, that would be tossed to a real COB? What's the easiest way to get someone back aboard the boat (swim platform, folding ladder, etc.)?

to return. Because accidents and mechanical problems have a way of unsettling plans, telling someone your *float plan* ensures that someone on shore will know if you don't return on time and can notify the proper authorities to start looking for you.

A float plan can be as simple as a note that provides your name, a description of your boat (including its name, color scheme, and state registration number), a brief outline of where you plan to boat during the day, and when you expect to return to the dock or boat ramp. It should also include the name and phone number of someone to call, such as a family member or neighbor, if you haven't returned by a certain time. You can file a float plan simply by telling your neighbor when you expect to be home, or you can leave a note with the dockmaster at your marina. If you trailered your powerboat to a public ramp, you can leave a float plan in an envelope tucked under the windshield wiper of your car.

FIRST-AID EQUIPMENT AND KNOWING HOW TO USE IT

A working knowledge of first-aid basics is critical out on the water, and it can keep minor injuries from turning into major ones. For comprehensive first-aid instructions, I recommend contacting your local Red Cross office for a copy of their excellent and easy-to-use handbook. And if you haven't attended a Red Cross first-aid and CPR course within the last few years, I strongly suggest you attend one as soon as possible. These courses are held in virtually every community across the country.

When choosing a **first-aid kit**, select one that is specifically intended to address the injuries that can occur on the water, possibly far from land and professional assistance.

A basic first-aid kit for powerboaters should include, at a minimum, a copy of the Red Cross first-aid manual, aspirin, acetaminophen or ibuprofen, sunburn ointment, antihistamine tablets, eye wash, alcohol wipes, Betadine wipes, emergency shears, tweezers, gauze pads, a variety of gauze bandages and adhesive bandages, a dozen cotton swabs, a roll of adhesive tape, a dozen surgical gloves, a CPR mask, a splint, rehydration salts, a survival blanket, and whatever specific medication you or any of your passengers take on a regular basis. Two firms that provide comprehensive first-aid kits that are well suited for boaters are Skynda—makers of the very comprehensive 2-pound Trek-Kit, which can address anything from chipped teeth to basic surgery and comes packaged in a waterproof case—and Atwater Carey, which offers a wide range of first-aid kits.

PERSONAL COMFORT

Some would say that being comfortable on a boat is a relative thing, since even the largest boats can tend to be bumpy places during heavy weather and desert islands on hot days. But there are many ways to make your powerboat a comfortable, fun place.

The first thing to do is pay attention to the weather and act accordingly. For example, if you're boating in the winter, slip on gloves and a scarf. If it's a blisteringly hot day out, put up the boat's *bimini top*, a one-piece canvas top that will shield you from the sun's rays. If you feel yourself becoming overheated, get out of the sun, splash cool water on your face, and drink some cool water, fruit juice, or sport drink. If possible, avoid colas or coffee since they contain caffeine, a diuretic. Beer and other alcoholic beverages also act as a diuretic—reason enough to avoid them when you're overheated—but more important, mixing alcohol and boating is a bad idea overall. You need all your faculties while you're operating your powerboat, so save the cocktails for after you're off the water for the day. Your passengers and your boat will appreciate it if you do.

When it's time for food, you can either tie up at a handy waterfront restaurant or eat snacks you've brought along. When planning meals afloat, keep the backyard barbecue in mind as a model and keep things simple, with items that require minimal preparation and handling. Apples, bananas, sandwiches, and carrot sticks work well and won't leave you with dirty dishes. Avoid serving greasy foods that could lead to queasy stomachs and exacerbate feelings of seasickness.

Also related to comfort, be aware of the ease with which your guests take to the water. Pay attention to how they're doing; just because you're having a great time doesn't mean they aren't scared, uncomfortable, tired, hungry, nauseous, or all of the above. In addition to being the captain, you are also the host, so don't lose sight of the niceties you'd observe back on dry land. If one of your guests is not reacting well to being out on the water, you may need to cut your cruise short to get her back on dry land. Make sure there's enough comfortable seating for everyone on board and that everyone has something to hold onto when the boat is going fast or when you hit another boat's wake. If there are smokers aboard, make sure they sit where their cigarettes won't bother other guests.

> "I love being out on my boat, but because it doesn't have a head, I know where all the waterfront restaurants, marinas, and fuel docks are with clean rest rooms."
>
> —Jayna Bollinger, Davie, Florida

Privacy and personal hygiene

Even large powerboats can begin to feel cramped at times because there's only so far you can go, and boats shorter than 30 feet can become downright tiny when you feel the need for privacy. If the boat has a cabin, it isn't considered rude to excuse yourself for a privacy break. If you're driving and you notice one of your guests seems edgy or uncomfortable, you might suggest she go below for a little while. The exception would be if she's feeling queasy, in which case it would better to let her go forward to the bow or find a corner aft near the transom for a privacy timeout. One reason some women have bad first experiences on a powerboat is this lack of privacy. If you feel queasy, you can go sit quietly in a corner, but if you become ill, everyone else on the boat will know.

It's always a good idea to use the rest room before leaving the dock, even if you don't think you have to, and to avoid diuretics like caffeinated and alcoholic beverages. Another way to deal with nature's call is to be prepared to duck into the closest waterfront restaurant or marina if there is one nearby. If you're cruising on the ocean or a large lake, the closest rest room could be several hours away. If the powerboat is large enough to have a *head*, now commonly referred to as an *MSD* (marine sanitation device), it's just a matter of excusing yourself for a few moments to go below.

If you are in a zero-discharge area (check with local authorities—all of Rhode Island is so designated) or within 3 miles of any coastline, you may not discharge any sewage from the boat, which means either waiting until you are ashore or having a bucket or other receptacle available. A one-time-use feminine sanitary device is another option. Stow tissues or disposable wipes in resealable plastic bags to dispose of ashore.

The situation becomes more complicated if you are on the water while menstruating, but even this is no excuse to stay on land. At such times, let everyone on board know about how long the boat will be out. Menstruating women should wear extra protection and carry ample supplies of tampons or pads, plus moist towelettes and resealable plastic bags. Have a couple oversize

• •

"**W**hen I was pregnant with my second child, I went out on my parent's cabin cruiser. I had been feeling huge and clumsy, but as soon as we left the dock and I took the controls, I suddenly felt like a skinny ballerina. It was mentally and physically refreshing, and I wish I'd discovered it sooner."

—Cindy Margolis, Hollywood, Florida

• •

towels for a friend to hold to give you some privacy if the powerboat doesn't have a cabin. Whether the "head" on the boat is a bucket or an MSD, stow used supplies in plastic bags, which you can later dispose of on land.

The head on a boat is different than rest rooms on shore, so if you're not sure how to use it, ask first. Most marine heads rely on a system of valves that let water in and then need to be pumped in order to flush the waste out. Most boats have a *holding tank* for onboard wastes, which can be emptied at a marina; others may pump waste directly into the water. Pumping waste overboard is only legal if you are several miles offshore and should never be done when there are swimmers near the boat.

Pregnancy and disability concerns

Within certain reasonable constraints, pregnancy isn't necessarily a reason to avoid being on the water. The final authority on the matter should always be your physician, but within her parameters and as long as you only boat in calm waters during good weather and you're comfortable moving around on the boat, there's no reason you can't keep boating for the majority of your term.

Powerboats seem to promote well-being; the feeling of control and self-confidence that comes with operating a powerboat is exhilarating and exciting. But one of the best things about boating, and powerboats specifically, is the fact that even persons with physical impairments can safely operate them. Because the only controls are the steering wheel and throttle, wheelchair-bound boaters can drive a boat without any problem. For other impairments, there are solutions; you may need to make a few concessions or recruit helpful crew, but the bottom line is that you can operate your own boat, so don't let any disability slow you down.

Seasickness and how to prevent it

Seasickness can range from a mild case of queasiness to full-blown agony that has you pleading for relief. Luckily, there are many ways to avoid this malady and many more to ease its discomfort. Seasickness is most commonly a reaction to your body's seeking equilibrium. Many women who have inner-ear infections, including powerboaters with years of experience, find themselves feeling seasick as their bodies try to sort out the conflicting feeling of being on a moving vessel in the water. Another potential cause is not being able to see the horizon, which can happen during a storm or if you're down below. Drinking the night before a cruise can leave your stomach jittery, as can eating greasy meals and even being overly hungry or thirsty.

Whatever the cause of seasickness, the first step is to get the person up on deck in the fresh air, preferably with a breeze in her face. Have her concentrate on the horizon and breathe deeply, which reestablishes the body's bearings and might be all that's required for relief. Sipping ginger ale or seltzer water usually helps, as does eating a few saltine crackers to settle a stomach. I know quite a few women who rely on acupressure wristbands, which are available at many marine stores, whereas others use over-the-counter medications like Dramamine or patches worn behind the ear (although some of these can cause drowsiness). One of the better ways to avoid seasickness or quickly cure it is to give the person a turn driving the boat; the act of concentrating on operating the boat is often very effective at getting your passenger beyond her initial queasiness.

Chapter 9

BASIC MAINTENANCE AND MINOR REPAIRS

HOW TO TELL WHETHER YOUR POWERBOAT IS OPERATING PROPERLY

Powerboats may seem to be a complex mass of moving parts, but they're actually pretty simple machines. Most problems can quickly be traced to the engine, propeller, steering, or electrical systems. After only a short time of using your boat, you will be able to tell if something isn't operating as it should be.

To stay on top of potential problems, use your intuition, talk to your mechanic or dealer, and take a close look at the boat yourself. For example, if the boat seems to be acting sluggish and you normally keep it stored on a trailer, look at the bottom to see whether there are barnacles growing there that can reduce speed. Or, open an access port to check the bilge to see whether it's holding water, which at 8 pounds per gallon can quickly weigh down even the fastest powerboat.

There are other possibilities to consider. Has the engine been tuned lately, or is it difficult to start and has a lot of smoke coming from the exhaust? Do the lights and radio work, or do they sometimes flicker on and off mysteriously? This could mean a frayed wire that needs to be repaired. If a loud horn suddenly sounds, this is most likely the engine overheating alarm, often caused by a plastic bag or other floating trash wrapping itself around the propeller or lower half of the outboard or stern drive, clogging the intakes. By paying attention to how the boat performs and sounds when everything is working properly, you'll be able to tell when it isn't. If in doubt,

TROUBLESHOOTING ENGINE PROBLEMS

Several situations can cause even the best-maintained powerboat to either malfunction or to stop running altogether. Luckily, they're fairly easy to diagnose and in most cases, to fix.

Symptom	Cause	Cure
engine won't start	dead battery	jump-start or recharge battery
engine won't start	no fuel or clogged filter	add fuel or replace fuel filter
engine runs rough	bad gas, water in fuel, or fouled spark plugs	add gas additive or change spark plugs
engine suddenly stops	no fuel or clogged filter	add fuel or replace filter
lights don't work	bad fuse or bulb	replace bulb or fuse
outboard engine runs, but boat won't move	loose propeller	check propeller shear pin
engine becomes sluggish or stops	clogged prop	check and clear prop of debris such as weeds or fishing line

take the boat to a mechanic as soon as possible to prevent a minor problem from becoming a major one.

If you're out on the water when a problem arises, first try to get your boat safely tied alongside a dock. Then you can try to determine what happened. The first thing to do is make sure you haven't inadvertently run out of fuel. Next, check the electrical system. Are your navigation lights working? How about the radio? By a process of elimination, you can ascertain what isn't wrong, which makes it easier to figure out what is. If the problem is a simple one, such as a blown fuse, you can probably fix it yourself and be back on your way. If you can't find the problem, call a marine towing firm to tow you to your marina.

CHOOSING A GOOD MECHANIC

Finding a good boat mechanic is as important to your boat's health as finding a good doctor is to your physical well-being. Sometimes it can be as easy as taking your powerboat to the local dealership or asking other powerboaters where they have their boats worked on. Location can be an issue, too, such as the convenience of a repair shop located on the waterfront. If you store your boat on a trailer, you have more options, since it's relatively easy to take your powerboat wherever the repair shop may be.

Finding a convenient repair facility is only half the battle; the most important part of choosing a good mechanic is finding one who listens to you, respects your requests, and provides quality work at reasonable prices. If practical, visit the repair shop before you need repairs, so you can

SIMPLE MAINTENANCE TASKS AND REPAIRS

If you own your own powerboat, you should know how to do simple repairs and maintenance tasks.

Task	Difficulty Level	How-To Hint	Time
replace bulbs or fuses	easy		5 minutes per bulb/fuse
add fuel additives	easy		5 minutes
add oil	easy		5 to 10 minutes
remove rust or corrosion	easy	use steel wool or a wire brush	15 minutes
remove stains from deck	fairly easy	use Davis FSR gel	15 minutes
replace fuel filter	fairly easy	screw off old, screw	15 minutes
change spark plugs	fairly easy	use spark plug wrench and plug gapping tool	60 minutes
repair gelcoat scratches	moderately hard	use scratch repair kit	30 minutes
remove scuff marks from hull	moderately hard	use hull cleaner or polishing compound	30 minutes to an hour
charge battery	moderately hard	remove cables from boat battery, attach battery charger to battery, remove when charged	3+ hours
repair torn upholstery	moderately hard	get an upholstery repair kit from West Marine or an auto parts store	several hours

see how the shop looks and how much attention the mechanics pay to their work. Don't assume that a clean shop is necessarily better than a messy shop; some of the best mechanics I know work in areas that look like they were just hit by a hurricane, yet they know where every nut and bolt is and they do quality, dependable work. While you're at the shop, ask for references and call them.

Most important, look for a mechanic that you feel comfortable entrusting with your powerboat. A good mechanic actually wants you to question every suspicious noise or operating quirk, because it makes it easier for him to keep the boat in first-class condition. If your mechanic makes it seem as if you're bothering him with silly questions, find a new one who values your boat as much as you do.

MINOR REPAIRS YOU CAN MAKE YOURSELF

The most common repairs needed on power-boats involve minor damage to the fiberglass exterior and bent propellers. These are two areas that require considerable experience, but there are many minor repairs you can do yourself. Doing your own repairs not only saves money, but it also builds self-confidence and that sense of being able to handle whatever comes your way—a strong characteristic of women powerboaters.

Electrical repairs

At some point, the bulbs and fuses in your powerboat's electrical system will need to be replaced. If a light stops working, it usually means either the bulb or the fuse has failed. Since it's easiest to check, start with the bulb.

Most bulbs are *bayonet style*, which means they have two prongs at the base to hold them in the socket. To replace bulbs, first use a screwdriver to remove the plastic cover, lay-ing it and the screws on a flat surface where they won't be lost or damaged. Make sure the bulb isn't too hot to touch. Try to let the bulb cool off before replacing it, but if you're out on the water you may need to replace it while under way, so use a towel to protect your fingers from being burned. Twist the bulb gently until you feel it loosen, and then just lift it out. Look at the fila-ment inside; if it's broken, the bulb is bad. The size of the bulb is engraved on its base; follow these numbers when purchasing a replacement.

If the filament looks fine, the problem could be a blown fuse. Luckily, fuses also are simple to replace. All but the smallest powerboats have fuses. The *fuse panel* is normally located close to the ignition switch and is a square-shaped panel, usually with a clear cover, with the fuses inside. First remove the fuse panel's plastic cover, and look for the fuse that is labeled "lights." If the fuse panel isn't labeled, you'll have to use trial and error to find the right one—pull the fuses out one at a time, looking at each to see whether the filament inside is broken. Take only one fuse out at a time to keep from accidentally putting them back in the wrong slot; fuses may all look alike, but they come in different amperages, which vary according to how much electricity passes through them, so it's important to replace them correctly.

If the bulb and the fuse are both OK, the problem could be a bad wire, and it may well be time to let a mechanic take over.

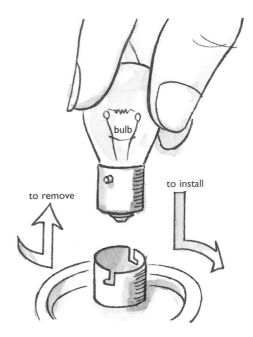

Many of the bulbs used in various lights on the boat are **bayonet style**. To remove these bulbs, twist the bulb sideways and then pull it out. To install a new bulb, set it in place and then twist sideways until it locks in place.

Engine repairs

What if your engine won't start? The first thing to do is make sure you haven't run out of fuel. If your boat has a gas gauge, check it and then double-check it by rapping your knuckles on the gas tank: a hollow sound indicates an empty tank, whereas a dull thud indicates gas (or diesel) in the tank. If there is gas in the tank, the problem could be a clogged fuel filter, which can be fixed by replacing the filter, or a crimped fuel line, which is more difficult to fix because you have to first locate the crimp.

Clogged fuel filters are fairly easy to replace: first, check your owner's manual to determine the location and type of the filter. *In-line filters* literally plug into the fuel line and are held in place by a hose clamp on either side. Turn the fuel shut-off valve, or if there isn't one, use a pair of locking pliers to crimp the fuel line closed, use a screwdriver to loosen the hose clamps, pull out the filter, put a replacement filter in, tighten the hose clamps, remove the locking pliers, and you're done. *Canister-type filters* screw in like a lightbulb and are just as easy to change. If your boat has a canister-type filter, close the fuel line with a shut-off valve or locking pliers, unscrew the filter, screw in a new one, and open the fuel line again.

Next check the battery. Can you turn on your navigation lights? If so, are they bright or dim (dim bulbs could be a sign of a battery too weak to start the engine). If you have bright lights and plenty of gas, your battery is probably OK and the problem lies elsewhere. It sounds basic, but also check the throttle. Many boats can't be started if the throttle is in either forward or reverse gear, but they crank right up once you slide the throttle into neutral.

Another reason for engines to run badly or not at all is dirty spark plugs. If the ends of the spark plugs become coated in soot from bad gasoline or from running the engine for extended periods of time at idle, they can cause the engine to malfunction. Determining whether a spark plug is bad is a simple process. Spark plugs have wires running from the top of them back to the engine—the trick is to look at only one at a time and to never unplug all the wires at once.

To remove the plugs one at a time, first unplug the top cap—it pops off when you apply a sideways motion. Using the spark plug wrench that should be in your basic tool kit, unscrew the plug. Once the plug is unscrewed, look at the bottom end—if it's black and oily or covered in gray ash, it could be too dirty to work properly. Your basic tool kit should have spare spark plugs of the same type and size you just removed. Spark plugs should be properly gapped, which you can do quickly with a simple device called a *gapping tool*. To install the new spark plug, first use your hand to screw it partially in. When it's finger-tight, use the spark plug wrench to snug it in, but not too tightly. Replace the rubber cap, and you should be ready to go.

Propeller repairs

How about if the engine runs great but you can't seem to go anywhere. It could be you've bent the propeller, broken the shear pin, or in an extreme case, maybe even knocked the propeller completely off. After turning off the engine, look at the propeller. If the prop looks OK and the edges aren't bent, it could be a broken *shear pin*, a short rod that holds the propeller to the drive

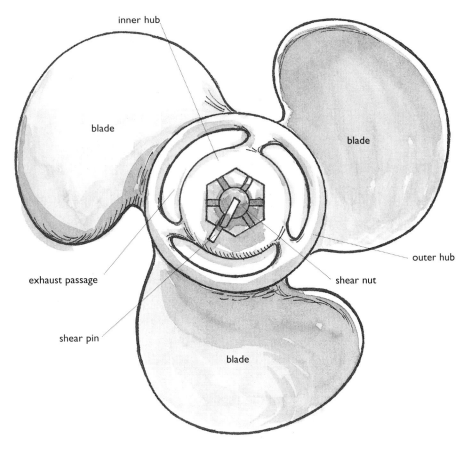

inner hub

blade

blade

outer hub

exhaust passage

shear nut

shear pin

blade

The main parts of a **propeller** are the blades, retaining nut, and a shear pin or nut. The shear pin or nut is designed to break first if the prop hits a hard object or runs aground. This stops the prop from spinning and saves the engine from serious damage.

shaft and keeps the propeller from being badly damaged if the prop hits a log or runs aground (the shear pin is designed to give way first). You can replace a shear pin (or *shear nut* on some boats) simply by sliding in a new one. If the propeller looks mangled or worse, however, call a marine towing firm to get you back to the dock where a mechanic can make proper repairs.

Upholstery repairs

Ripped or torn upholstery may not look pretty, but you can make fast, temporary repairs by carrying a roll of shrink-wrap tape in your boater's bag. Unlike duct tape, which is shiny silver, leaves a sticky residue, and can bake on so hard it can't be removed, shrink-wrap tape is available in white and is easy to remove. If you find a tear or rip in your boat's upholstery, just cover it with a strip of shrink-wrap tape. It isn't a permanent repair, but it will hold long enough for you to get to an upholstery repair shop.

MAINTENANCE SCHEDULE

Maintaining your boat by following this checklist is the best way to avoid problems.

Task	Daily	Monthly	Annually	After Each Cruise
check oil	✓			
inspect wiring		✓		
flush engine				✓
wash hull				✓
wax hull		✓		
check battery		✓		
add fuel additives			✓	
check bulbs/fuses		✓		
grease trailer bearings			✓	
renew registration			✓	
drain bilge				✓

High-lacquer hair spray acts as a barrier to moisture, preventing corrosion on engine parts and wiring

PREVENTIVE MAINTENANCE

You probably can guess how easy it is to get your boat dirty, but the good news is it's very simple to clean it and keep it clean. The majority of powerboats are constructed of fiberglass, which combines durability with good looks. Applying a protective coat of Star brite's marine polish with Teflon to your boat's hull takes about 20 minutes per 10 feet of boat length and provides a finish that repels dirt and water stains so cleaning the boat takes less time, makes the hull smoother so it moves through the water easier, and also looks good. The rule of thumb to polishing fiberglass (as with cars!) is if water won't bead on it, or does so in spots larger than a quarter, it's time to polish. While you're at it, apply a coat to all stainless and polished aluminum fitting and rails to keep them clean and spot-free.

By taking a few minutes to clean your boat at the end of every cruise, you can avoid having to spend hours cleaning accumulated grime and stains. And while you're cleaning, take the time to look at the condition of all your power-boat's parts, fixing things as you see them, rather than waiting for them to become an issue. For instance, when you notice the oil level is low in your outboard's oil reservoir, take a moment to fill it—if you notice a loose wire, fix it instead of putting it off until later. Any maintenance you do now will take less time than if you wait until it becomes a problem.

A soft bristle brush, a hose, and a bucket of soapy water are all the tools you need to clean fiberglass—never use dishwashing detergent, which can etch the surface. Starting at the highest parts of the boat, use the soap and scrub downward, rinsing thoroughly every few minutes to prevent the soap from drying. As you rinse, lay a towel over the instruments and electronics to keep them from getting wet, which can cause fogging. A scrub brush is especially useful to loosen grime from upholstery or nylon fenders, or to lift stains from nonskid deck sur-

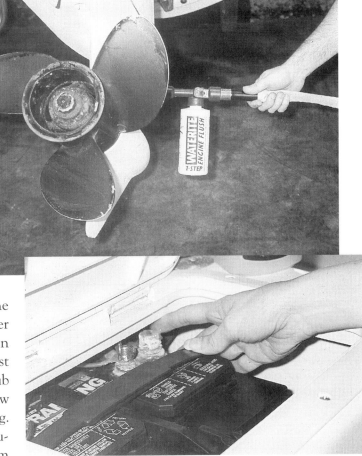

Top: **Flushing the engine** must be done immediately after every saltwater cruise to prevent the buildup of corrosive materials that can damage the engine. **Bottom:** One of the simplest do-it-yourself maintenance jobs is coating the boat's **battery terminals** with petroleum jelly to prevent them from becoming corroded.

faces. While you're scrubbing the boat, don't forget to flush the engine, especially if you've been boating in salt or brackish waters. Use WD-40 to spray a protective film over battery terminals after you've checked the water levels, and you're done.

A clean boat runs better, and since it shouldn't take more than an hour to spiff it up, this is the easiest maintenance you can do to keep your boat looking and running like new.

Flushing the engine

If you have an inboard engine that's equipped with a radiator, make sure it's full of *coolant* (a mix of water and antifreeze). However, most boat engines use the water they run in to keep cool, so you should never start your boat's engines unless the boat is in the water or you've attached a water source to the engine, a process called *flushing* the engine. If you boat in salt water, it's especially important to flush the motor after each cruise in order to rinse all the salt out of the engine. You can safely start the engine with the boat on the trailer or out of the water by using a *motor flusher*, which looks like a pair of Mickey Mouse ears and fits over the water intakes on the engine's lower unit. Attach the flusher to a garden hose to supply freshwater, and run the engine for about five minutes to thoroughly clean its cooling system.

Watching the oil

Every time you fill the boat's fuel tank, check the oil dipstick and add oil if the level drops below the "OK" mark. Gasoline engines are either *two-cycle* or *four-cycle* (sometimes also called *two-stroke* or *four-stroke*). Most inboard engines are four-cycle (the same as a car engine), with a separate oil reservoir for regular automotive-type engine oil. If the engine is an outboard, it can be either a four-cycle or a two-cycle .

A two-cycle engine burns oil along with the gas; if it has an automatic oil-injection system, all you have to do is keep the reservoir filled with *TCW-3 oil* (TCW stands for two-cycle, water-cooled), which is specifically formulated for use in two-cycle outboard engines. If the engine doesn't have an oil-injection system, you'll need to add TCW-3 directly to the gas tank, simply by pouring it in. Adding too much TCW-3 (check your owner's manual for the proper amount) will keep the engine from running well, produce a lot of white smoke, and could clog the spark plugs. If your boat uses TCW-3, make sure you have a spare bottle stowed on the boat in case the fuel dock has run out. Don't even think about trying to run the engine on plain gas—it can cause damage requiring costly repairs.

If the outboard engine is a four-cycle, all you need to do is keep the separate oil reservoir full. Most outboard motor manufacturers are now introducing four-cycle models because they use less fuel by burning it more efficiently, and they produce less exhaust and thus less pollution. Four-cycle outboards tend to be heavier and more expensive than a similarly sized two-cycle, but they also run quieter and smoother. Recently, some states have considered banning two-cycle engines because of all the unburnt fuel in their exhaust.

Keeping your boat clean

Nothing is as sleek and beautiful as a new powerboat, which explains why so

Many **inflatable boats** can actually be stored in a garage or large closet, and transported in the trunk of a car.

many people end up purchasing one at a boat show where all the new models are laid out in gorgeous displays. But a better option than purchasing a new boat every year is to learn how to keep your own boat looking new. Although it sounds obvious, the easiest way to keep a boat clean is to not let it get dirty, which is best done by keeping it covered.

The best way to store a boat is indoors, and many marinas offer what they call "stack and rack" inside storage for powerboats up to about 30 feet long. The marina uses a forklift to raise the boat out of the water and transport it inside a large barn-like building, where it is placed on a multilevel rack secure from the elements. Inside storage isn't for everyone, though, because it can be expensive, the marina may not be conveniently located, the facility might not have room for your boat, or your boat may be longer than 30 feet.

Even without indoor storage, you can still protect your boat by using a cover made of a protective material like Sunbrella, which is the same material used to manufacture bimini tops for boats. Using a boat cover protects your boat from dust and grit and prevents the fiberglass hull and vinyl cushions from fading due to sun exposure. I use a Sunbrella fabric cover made by Taylor that completely wraps over my 15-foot Boston Whaler; it takes about 10 minutes to slip the cover in place and secure it, but when I take it off, the boat is as clean as when I last washed it, which saves me at least an hour of work.

Top: **Custom covers** that completely encase your boat are the best protection against grime and UV rays, which can quickly dull the finish. **Bottom:** Covering the lower unit of an outboard or stern drive when the boat is put away for **winter storage** is the most effective way to make sure it will still be clean in the spring.

Paying attention to your trailer

After you've launched your boat is the easiest time to check the trailer for corrosion, loose or cracked wires, loose license plate bolts, burned-out bulbs, loose bunks, or cracked rollers. Even if all the bulbs are working, at least once a season take them out (they twist out easily) and spray the base of the bulb and its socket with a moisture-displacing lubricant like WD-40. Next, liberally spray a waxy lubricant like TaskMaster all over the axle,

WINTER STORAGE

Unless you live in a state like Florida or Arizona where it's warm enough to boat year-round, you'll need to prepare your boat for storage during the winter. Unless your boat is very large, you are best storing it out of the water for the winter months. If you have a trailer, use it, and if not, arrange for the boat to be stored on a cradle at a local marina or boatyard. Storing the boat indoors may cost more, but it's worth it in terms of maintaining the boat in good condition.

To prepare the boat for winter storage,

1. Use a fogging agent to protect the engine from corrosion during storage.
2. Drain all the water lines from the engine and plumbing system to prevent freeze damage.
3. Disconnect the batteries and remove them to a garage or other safe, warm place.
4. Top off the fuel tanks to remove any air pockets that can cause condensation, which leads to corrosion and sludge.
5. Add a fuel stabilizer additive that maintains the octane level while absorbing water.
6. Remove the boat's canvas, all electronic gear like depthfinders, and any personal items, storing them inside a garage or other protected area.
7. Cover the boat with shrink-wrap plastic to seal out dirt and dust.

Following these steps will help ensure your boat will look as good in the spring as it did when you put it away for the winter. If all this seems like too much bother, do what I did and move to Florida!

wheels, trailer hitch coupler, metal winch cable, and any moving parts to protect them from rust and corrosion, and rub paraffin on the bunks. If you boat in salt or brackish waters and a freshwater hose is handy, rinse the trailer to sluice away any salt to keep it from building up and causing rust. When you retrieve the boat, inspect the winch cable or strap for cuts or frays, and make sure it goes on the winch spool without overlapping.

Spending a little time after every cruise or when the boat has not been used for a while will make the boat last longer and look better.

Chapter 10

POWERBOATING WITH FRIENDS AND FAMILY

At this point, you may be wondering how to share your interest in powerboating with other people in your life. You may need information on how to find other women to share your powerboating experiences with. I'll address this here as well as give you some tips on just how far you can take powerboating for adventure and enjoyment.

SHARING THE JOYS OF POWERBOATING

Whether you're brand-new to powerboating or have spent the past 20 years at the helm of your own boats, it's natural to want to share the experience with others. Perhaps because it's a healthy adventure enjoyed outside in the fresh air and sunshine, boating is a social activity that goes best with company. There are those who prefer their own company out on the water, but the majority of boaters enjoy boating with a group, reveling in the excitement with one another.

When you're new to a sport or have just moved to a new area, it can seem difficult to find others to share your adventures. If you're looking to meet other women powerboaters, the best place to start is where the boats are. There is a camaraderie that makes our sport special, and it extends to anyone showing enthusiasm and excitement. Enrolling in a Power Squadrons course

· ·

"**W**hen I moved from Sacramento to Fort Lauderdale, I didn't know anyone there who boated. I signed up for a boating safety class, even though I'd attended a Power Squadrons course years before. I met a lot of fun people in the class, and within a week, I was back out on the water."

—Stephie Bostwick, Fort Lauderdale, Florida

· ·

is one great way to gain practical knowledge and to meet others who share your excitement. Even if you've previously attended a boating safety course, there's always more to learn; by taking a re-fresher course, you can pick up additional boating knowledge while spending time around other power-boaters.

If you're at a boat ramp, feel free to talk to the people launching and retrieving their boats. Unless they're at a critical stage of the process, such as backing the trailer into the water, most powerboaters are glad to talk and explain what they're doing. You probably won't garner many invitations to go for a cruise, but just by staying out of the way and watching, you'll absorb useful information without even trying.

Many communities have small-boat clubs that welcome guests and new members. These aren't yacht clubs, which tend to have more of a social focus, but rather clubs made up of active powerboaters who get more excited about building a new boat ramp than planning holiday parties. Most communities have local marine publications that are published weekly or monthly, many of which provide a list of clubs in the area and a schedule of upcoming events. By attending meetings and seminars, you'll be around people who share your passion for the water, which gets you half the way toward making new friends.

Another great way to share the joys of powerboating is to tell your friends, family, and coworkers about it. A few unobtrusive maritime accessories displayed on your desk or wearing a shirt on dress-down day that bears a manufacturer's logo tells the world you're a powerboater and serves as an effective icebreaker for discovering which coworkers or acquaintances share your love for being out on a boat. Once they've learned that

Boating offers a great way to get to know colleagues and neighbors in a different context.

your air of healthy self-confidence comes from your experiences on the water, some people will be intrigued and start asking about how they can become power-boaters too; don't be surprised to find others asking for invitations to go boating with you!

Attending local boat shows is a fun way to meet fellow boaters as well as see what's new in boat designs and products. The people working the various booths and displays are there to talk with you,

Keeping your boat at a marina gives you a sense of community.

so feel free to stop and ask questions. This is a good time to become acquainted with the staff of local stores; when they recognize you in the store after meeting you at a boat show, you'll discover that you have graduated to the status of a regular customer and will find yourself treated like an old friend. Local boat clubs usually will have a booth at these shows in order to attract new members. Find out if you can attend a meeting or event as a guest, and you're on your way.

BRINGING THE WHOLE FAMILY

Boating is an activity that the whole family can enjoy, from the youngest kids to the grandparents—and don't forget the dog! When planning who to bring along on cruises, my main criteria are the person's health and what she is expecting to gain from the experience. For instance, children tend to have short attention spans, and a long cruise with few or no interim stops can seem like a prison sentence to them. On the other hand, many adults are content to sit back and quietly enjoy the passing scenery, stopping only to refuel or take time out for a meal. By keeping the needs of your passengers in mind, you can make sure everyone has an enjoyable time. Don't try to include too many activities—such as fishing, diving, and sight-seeing—on your cruises. You'll get more enjoyment and relaxation by keeping things simple, and you will have fewer preparations to make and less stuff to bring along.

Plan ahead by bringing enough drinks and snacks to keep everyone comfortable, and be ready

KEEPING KIDS SAFE ON YOUR BOAT

I pretty much grew up on a boat, so I took for granted the heathy lifestyle of sun, water, and general outdoor fun. In order to make my boat safe for children, I am unbending on the rule that all kids wear PFDs at all times they are on the boat or the dock—the coast guard says that the easiest way to prevent injuries or drownings is to have everyone wear PFDs, a guideline that's doubly important when it comes to children.

Being out in the warm sunshine with the world floating past can excite any child, so you need to make sure they understand what they can and cannot do. No matter how many other boats you see doing it, never let children sit on the bow with their feet dangling over the side—it looks like fun, but can turn to tragedy in an instant if they fall over in the path of the prop or hit their head on the hull. Don't let them run on the boat, and make sure they wear proper boat shoes or sneakers with nonskid soles—flip-flops can cause slips and won't protect little toes from being stubbed on exposed cleats.

(continued on next page)

"I first went boating when I was five years old, and I've been on boats ever since. It was a great way to grow up, seeing nature up close and personal, and I think it makes for healthy kids."

—Mary Martin, Cape Hatteras, North Carolina

for unscheduled rest-room stops along the way. During the Christmas holiday season, I like to take friends and family out to see the various decorations put up along the waterways, on homes as well as on other boats. Many waterfront communities host Christmas boat parades, with awards given out for best design or most spirited crew. For example, every December, Fort Lauderdale hosts the Winterfest Boat Parade, which is televised nationally.

Kids

To keep kids happy afloat—after first fitting them with their own PFDs—get them involved in the cruise, asking them to serve as lookouts to help you spot upcoming channel markers and other boat traffic. Teaching them the names of the various types of boats or the basics of the rules of the road not only keeps them entertained, it also helps them enter the world of powerboating. Stearns makes an inflatable underwater viewer that entertains kids and adults for hours as they watch the world beneath the water passing along.

How young is too young to go boating? That's a question for your family physician, but my personal inclination is that as long as a child is old enough to swim, agrees to wear a PFD the entire time she is on the water, and can be trusted to behave properly, she can go out on my boat. My rule of thumb is the younger the child (as well as the older the guest), the shorter the cruise. If there is any doubt as to the wisdom of

It's easy to get kids to wear PFDs by letting them choose styles and colors that suit them and making sure their choices fit right.

There is no age limit for enjoying the world that opens up when you step aboard a powerboat.

KEEPING KIDS SAFE ON YOUR BOAT
• • • • • • • • • • • • • • • • • • •

(continued from previous page)
In addition to boat shoes and PFDs that fit right (the coast guard requires you to have PFDs that actually fit each person on board), each child should also wear sunscreen to prevent sunburn. Kids can become seasick quickly, so keep ginger ale on hand to help quell the queasiness. By paying attention to your smaller passengers, you can make sure they have a good cruise, and you'll find having them along makes it better for you as well.

taking anyone out on the boat, play it safe and don't do it. Having kids on your powerboat is a serious responsibility, but as long as you keep them in PFDs, they don't run around on wet slippery decks, and you don't let them sit on the bow with their feet dangling over, spending time out on the water in the fresh air and sunshine on a boat is a wonderful way to spend a day—and much healthier than a day spent at the mall.

If the children you're taking on the boat aren't yours, find out before the cruise whether they have any special medical needs, are allergic to certain bug bites, or are taking prescription drugs. These children will be your responsibility the whole time you're away from the dock, so you must be aware of any special needs they may have.

Pets

My dachshunds are regular passengers on my boat, and they enjoy being out on the water as much as I do. Most pets are welcome additions; you'll find out very quickly whether your dog or cat wants to become a powerboater. If the pet is hesitant, don't force the issue, or you may both regret it later.

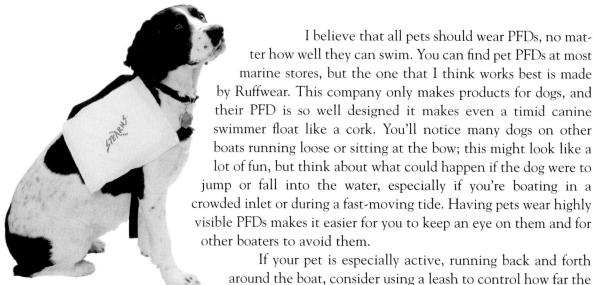

Strong swimmers or not, all pets should have their own properly sized PFDs.

I believe that all pets should wear PFDs, no matter how well they can swim. You can find pet PFDs at most marine stores, but the one that I think works best is made by Ruffwear. This company only makes products for dogs, and their PFD is so well designed it makes even a timid canine swimmer float like a cork. You'll notice many dogs on other boats running loose or sitting at the bow; this might look like a lot of fun, but think about what could happen if the dog were to jump or fall into the water, especially if you're boating in a crowded inlet or during a fast-moving tide. Having pets wear highly visible PFDs makes it easier for you to keep an eye on them and for other boaters to avoid them.

If your pet is especially active, running back and forth around the boat, consider using a leash to control how far the pet can travel. Always make sure the animal has plenty of cool water and a shady, comfortable place to rest.

TAKING VACATIONS AFLOAT AND EXTENDED CRUISES

The nice thing about the sport of powerboating is that you can enjoy it wherever there is enough water to float your boat. Being on the water opens up a whole new world. Even if you've spent your whole life in one community or city, if you haven't yet spent time on its waters, there is an entirely different side waiting to be discovered. By spending vacations afloat, you'll have the opportunity to savor new worlds.

Vacations afloat can range from spending long weekend days puttering around in a small outboard powerboat to chartering a large powerboat for an extended cruise in an exotic destination. If you store your powerboat on a trailer, you can take it with you on vacations, using it to see new areas from a perspective few tourists enjoy or have access to. Because I live in Florida, there are few places I can go that don't offer boating opportunities, and I have learned the joy of bringing a boat along or renting one at my destination. If I'm traveling with friends and boating isn't the primary focus of the vacation, as long as the area has navigable waters, we'll still bring a small boat

"**F**or the past three years, a group of us have been taking bareboat charter vacations all over the Caribbean and the U.S. We all share expenses, so it ends up costing about the same as if we'd stayed at a nice hotel, but we have the freedom of a boat we can take wherever we want."

—Kaitlin Jorgesen, Miami, Florida

along to use for afternoon sight-seeing or to go out for dinner at a waterfront restaurant. While it isn't as simple as bringing along bicycles, the idea is similar—to be able to see more, enjoy more, and get more out of vacation time.

Chartering large power-boats is a great way for a group of people to combine the adventure of travel with time spent on the water. Powerboats ranging from 20-foot house-boats to 70-foot yachts can be chartered throughout the United States and all over the world. If you have the experience to operate a large powerboat, you can arrange a *bareboat charter*. With a bareboat charter, you're in charge of the boat and are responsible for supplying all food and provisions. Bareboats come equipped with everything you need, except food, fuel, and crew. Because you can share expenses, bareboats are a great way to keep costs down while getting hands-on experience operating a large powerboat in new and possi-

Top: Sometimes it's easier to get to your favorite waterfront restaurant by boat rather than by car. **Bottom:** Many waterfront hotels and resorts invite you to bring your boat along to use during your vacation.

bly exotic destinations. Owning a large powerboat requires a huge commitment of time and money, but by chartering one you pay only for the time you actually spend using the boat.

If you aren't comfortable operating a larger powerboat, another option is a *crewed charter*. With this option, all you have to do is pick a location and, when you arrive, a powerboat will be ready and waiting, fully prepared and staffed by a captain and (depending on the boat's size) perhaps even a cook and crew to handle the deck work. A crewed charter costs more than a bareboat, but one way to keep expenses down is to book a trip during the off-season.

The best way to find out about bareboat or crewed charters is to contact a yacht charter company. You'll find listings and advertisements for charter companies in the back sections of

ADVENTURES FROM YOUR BOAT

A powerboat opens up a whole new world that is denied to the landbound. Your boat lets you enjoy new activities such as fishing where the fish are and diving in areas that are otherwise inaccessible. Even if you're intimately familiar with a particular area, seeing it from the vantage of the water presents it in a whole new light. A boat lets you go waterskiing or explore small islands where you can enjoy a barbecue or camp overnight. On well-marked inland waterways, a small 21-foot boat is all you need for extensive touring via the water, camping on the boat or staying in waterfront accommodations along the way. For shorter jaunts, taking friends and family to your favorite waterfront restaurant by boat makes even the best meal that much better.

Nature lovers will be particularly pleased at how close they can get to species of birds and wildlife they never saw from shore. A mask and snorkel let you explore the world beneath the waves, and if the lure is strong enough, a scuba tank takes you even deeper. During the winter holidays, many waterfront communities display decorations that are visible only from the water. And no matter how crowded the

Only keep fish you intend to eat, carefully releasing all other fish to be caught again another day.

beach may be on a sunny day, your boat always has enough room for you and your friends to sunbathe in uncrowded comfort. The possibilities for what you can do on your boat are only limited by your imagination.

popular powerboating magazines. Feel free to ask the charter company for references, or get recommendations from friends who have chartered powerboats in the past.

FURTHER ADVENTURES

Your powerboat is more than a passport to new scenery and new friendships. The list of what you can do with your powerboat is limited only by your imagination. Your boat can take you places that you can only reach via the water, and you'll be amazed at just how many adventures are out there. Even a simple weekend picnic lunch on a deserted island in the middle of a busy waterway can be a grand adventure. Take part in floating parties, or *raft-ups*, in which a group of boats throw out anchors and tie up next to one another for a party. These gatherings are a great way to spend time with other powerboaters who share your love of the water and boats.

In addition to the full-scale vacations afloat described earlier, you'll also discover that just taking the boat out for a short cruise can be a mini-vacation in itself. By taking you away even briefly from the stress and aggravations of life on dry land, a short cruise can refresh and reenergize you.

You can also find out when the local boat clubs are holding *flotillas* or other organized waterfront activities that you can attend. As a boater, if you scuba dive or fish or if you just want to

Top: **Rafting up** (securing two or more boats together with lines) with friends is a great way to spend a weekend, or you can attend any of the many organized raft-ups around the country during the summer. **Bottom:** A chartered **sportfisherman** is ideal for vacationing with friends since it has plenty of room—and a two-story view!

A flotilla is an organized gathering of powerboats that join together to travel to specific destinations. They're a great way for powerboaters—experts or novices—to vacation on their boats.

find out whether you'd enjoy taking up these hobbies, you will find yourself welcome at clubs catering to these sports, where many members may not have their own boat and would love to share expenses and adventures with you.

You're on your way to an adventure that will continue to be rewarding and exciting for the rest of your life. I wish you good luck, good friends, and good weather—and don't forget to wave when you see me on the water!

The more you learn about powerboating, the more you'll want to continue to add to your store of knowledge. The following listings will help you discover the joys of boating and expand your horizons.

BOOKS

Bottomley, Tom. *Boatman's Handbook: The New Look-It-Up Book*. New York: Hearst Marine Books, 1988.

Buehler, George. *The Troller Yacht Book: A Powerboater's Guide to Crossing Oceans without Getting Wet or Going Broke*. New York: W. W. Norton & Co., 1999.

Cantrell, Debra. *Changing Course: A Woman's Guide to Choosing the Cruising Life*. Camden ME: International Marine, 2000.

Caswell, Christopher, and James E. Mitchell. *The Illustrated Book of Basic Boating*. New York: Hearst Marine Books, 1990.

De Neergard, Helene Gaillet. *The Boat Book*. Stamford CT: Westcott Cove Publishing, 1994.

Hinz, Earl R., and Richard R. Rhodes. *The Complete Book of Anchoring and Mooring*. Centreville MD: Cornell Maritime Press, 1999.

Lamy, J. P. *Boating Magazine's Insider's Guide to Buying a Powerboat*. Camden ME: International Marine, 2000.

McMullen, Alex. *Motor Boating: A Motor Boating and Yachting Book*. Alpine NY: Fernhurst Books, 1998.

Spurr, Daniel. *Heart of Glass: Fiberglass Boats and the Men Who Made Them*. Camden ME: International Marine, 2000.

Vigor, John. *The Practical Mariner's Book of Knowledge: 420 Sea-Tested Rules of Thumb for Almost Every Boating Situation*. Camden ME: International Marine, 1994.

Wing, Charlie. *The Liveaboard Report: A Boat Dweller's Complete Guide to What Works and What Doesn't.* Camden ME: International Marine, 1997.

Yetman, David S. *Boater's Book of Nautical Terms.* Enola PA: Bristol Fashion, 1998.

Seamanship, weather, the ocean

Carr, Michael. *Weather Predicting Simplified: How to Read Weather Charts and Satellite Images.* Camden ME: International Marine, 1999.

Cassidy, John. *The Klutz Book of Knots: How to Tie the World's 25 Most Useful Hitches, Ties, Wraps, and Knots: A Step-by-Step Manual.* Palo Alto CA: Klutz Press, 1985.

Eldridge Tide and Pilot Book (2000).

Hubbard, Richard. *Boater's Bowditch: The Small-Craft American Practical Navigator.* Camden ME: International Marine, 2000.

Kotsch, William J. *Weather for the Mariner.* Annapolis MD: Naval Institute Press, 1983.

Leonard, Beth. *The Voyager's Handbook: The Essential Guide to Blue Water Cruising.* Camden ME: International Marine, 1998.

Maloney, Elbert S., and Charles Frederic Chapman. *Chapman Piloting: Seamanship and Small Boat Handling.* 62nd ed. New York: Hearst Books, 1996.

Rousmaniere, John. *The Annapolis Book of Seamanship.* New York: Simon & Schuster, 1999.

U.S. Coast Guard. *International Regulations for Preventing Collisions at Sea* (COLREGS). Washington DC: U.S. Government Printing Office. Downloadable document available at <www.uscg.mil/ vtm/pages/rules.htm>.

U.S. Coast Guard. *Navigation Rules: International–Inland.* Washington DC: U.S. Government Printing Office, 1996. Downloadable document available at <www.uscg.mil/ vtm/pages/rules.htm>.

Travel and adventure by boat

Evergreen Pacific Pub. *Evergreen Pacific Cruising Guide: Washington Waters.* Seattle WA: Evergreen Pacific Pub., 1994.

Horn, Les. *Through Europe at Four Knots: A Tale of Boating Mayhem and Family Adventure.* Camden ME: International Marine, 2000.

Kettlewell, John, and Leslie Kettlewell. *The International Marine Light List and Waypoint Guide: from Maine to Texas, including the Bahamas.* Camden ME: International Marine, 1997.

Ludmer, Larry H. *Cruising Alaska: A Traveller's Guide to Cruising Alaskan Waters and Discovering the Interior.* 4th ed. Leesburg VA: Hunter Pub., 1999.

Moeller, Jan, and Bill Moeller. *The Intracoastal Waterway: Norfolk to Miami: A Cockpit Cruising Handbook.* Camden ME: International Marine, 1997.

Simon, Alvah. *North to the Night: A Year in the Arctic Ice.* Camden ME: International Marine, 1999.

Smith, Richard Y., and Elizabeth Adams Smith. *Atlantic Cruising Club's Guide to East Coast Marinas.* Rye NY: Atlantic Cruising Club, 1997.

Stob, Ron, and Eva I. Stob. *"Honey, Let's Get a Boat . . . ": A Cruising Adventure of America's Great Loop.* Greenback TN: Raven Cove Pub., 1999.

Wilson, Mathew. *The Bahamas Cruising Guide.* Camden ME: International Marine, 1998.

Young, Claiborne S. *Cruising Guide to Eastern Florida.* 3rd ed. Gretna LA: Pelican Pub. Co., 1996.

Young, Claiborne S. *Power Cruising: The Complete Guide to Selecting, Outfitting, and Maintaining Your Power Boat.* Gretna LA: Pelican Pub. Co., 1999.

Repair and maintenance

Berrien, Allan. *Boating Magazine's The Boat Doctor.* Camden ME: International Marine, 1998.

Board, Sherri. *Boat Cosmetics Made Simple: How to Improve and Maintain a Boat's Appearance.* Irvine CA: Tug Press, 1993.

Brown, David G. *Hearst Marine Books Complete Guide to Boat Maintenance and Repair.* New York: Hearst Marine Books, 1993.

Burr, William M., Jr. *Boat Maintenance: The Essential*

Guide to Cleaning, Painting, and Cosmetics. Camden ME: International Marine, 2000.

Calder, Nigel. *Marine Diesel Engines: Maintenance, Troubleshooting, and Repair.* 2nd ed. Camden ME: International Marine, 1991.

Casey, Don. *100 Fast and Easy Boat Improvements.* Camden ME: International Marine, 1998.

Hewitt, Dick, and R. L. Hewitt. *Boat Engines: A Motor Boat and Yachting Book.* Alpine NY: Fernhurst Books, 1998.

Lindsey, Sandy. *Boating Magazine's Quick and Easy Boat Maintenance: 1,001 Time-Saving Tips.* Camden ME: International Marine, 1999.

Lipe, Karen S., and Cynthia Taylor Dax. *The Big Book of Boat Canvas: A Complete Guide to Fabric Work on Boats.* Camden ME: International Marine, 1991.

Nicolson, Ian, and Aan Nicolson. *The Boat Data Book.* 4th ed. Dobbs Ferry NY: Sheridan House, 1999.

Seddon, Don. *Diesel Troubleshooter.* Alpine NY: Fernhurst Books, 1999.

Streiffert, Bo, Dag Pike, and Loris Goring. *Modern Boat Maintenance: The Complete Fiberglass Boat Manual.* Dobbs Ferry NY: Sheridan House, 1994.

Vaitses, Allan H. *The Fiberglass Boat Repair Manual.* Camden ME: International Marine, 1988.

White, Peter. *The Outboard Troubleshooter.* Alpine NY: Fernhurst Books, 1998.

MAGAZINES

Boating
122 E. 42nd St., Suite 2211
New York NY 10168
212-455-1621
www.Boatingmag.com

Boating Life
460 N. Orlando Ave., Suite 200
Winter Park FL 32789
800-453-8877
www.boatinglifemag.com

Lakeland Boating
500 Davis St., Suite 1000
Evanston IL 60201
847-869-5400
www.lakelandboating.com

Motor Boating & Sailing
250 W. 55th St.
New York NY 10019
212-649-3059
www.motorboating.com

Offshore
220 Reservoir St., Suite 9
Needham MA 02494
781-449-6204
OFFeditor@aol.com

Powerboat
1691 Spinnaker Dr., Suite 206
Ventura CA 93001
805-639-2222
www.powerboatmag.com

Sea: America's Western Boating Magazine
P.O. Box 25859
Santa Ana CA 92799
888-732-7323
www.seamag.com

Southern Boating
1766 Bay Rd.
Miami Beach FL 33139
305-538-0700
sboating@southernboating.com
www.southernboating.com

Yachting
2 Park Ave.
New York NY 10016
800-999-0869
www.yachtingnet.com

VIDEOS

The Annapolis Book of Seamanship Videos
Boating Basics
Boating Magazine's Top 60 Boating Tips—Boat Handling
Boating Magazine's Top 60 Boating Tips—Navigation
Dinghies and Inflatables
GPS Guide for the Mariner
Modern Coastal Piloting
On the Water Boating Tips
Rules of the Road
VHF Made Easy
All of these videos are available from Bennett Marine Video, 2321 Abbot Kinney Blvd., Venice CA 90291, 800-733-8862, <*www.bennettmarine.com*>.

INTERNET SOURCES

BoatFacts Online, <*www.boatfacts.com*>
Boating.Com, <*www.boating.com*>
BoatSafe.com and BoatSafe Kids, <*www.boatsafe.com*>

BoatsandBoating.com,
    <*www.boatsandboating.com*>
iWaterways.com,
    <*www.iwaterways.com*>
MarinersGuide.com,
    <*www.marinersguide.com*>
U.S. Coast Guard Navigation
    Rules, <*www.uscg.mil/vtm/*
    pages/rules.htm>
Women in Scuba,
    <*www.womeninscuba.com*>

EQUIPMENT SOURCES

ACR Electronics, Inc.
5757 Ravenswood Rd.
Fort Lauderdale FL 33312
800-432-0227
www.acrelectronics.com

Bass Pro Shops/Offshore Angler
    Saltwater/Outdoor World
2500 E. Kearney
Springfield MO 65898
800-BASSPRO (800-227-7776)
www.basspro.com

Blue Water Books and Charts
1481 S.E. 17th St.
Fort Lauderdale FL 33316
954-763-6533; 800-942-2583
www.bluewaterweb.com

BoatLIFE
2081 Bridgeview Dr.
P.O. Box 71789
Charleston SC 29415-1789
800-382-9706
www.boatlife.com

BoatU.S. (Boat Owners Association
    of The United States)
880 S. Pickett St.
Alexandria VA 22304
800-568-0319
www.boatus.com

Garmin International, Inc.
1200 E. 151st St.
Olathe KS 66062
913-397-8200; 800-800-1020
www.garmin.com

Landfall Navigation
354 W. Putnam Ave.
Greenwich CT 06830
800-941-2219
www.landfallnav.com
Available products include *Eldridge
    Tide and Pilot Book.*

Weems and Plath
222 Severn Ave.
Annapolis MD 21403
410-263-6700
www.weems-plath.com.

West Marine
P.O. Box 50050
Watsonville CA 95077-5050
800-BOATING (800-262-8464)
www.westmarine.com

CLOTHING

Columbia Sportswear Co.
Attn: Consumer Services
P.O. Box 83239
Portland OR 97283-0239
800-547-8066
consumer_services@
    columbia.com
www.columbia.com/

Hook & Tackle Sportswear
6501 N.E. 2nd Court
Miami FL 33138
305-754-3255
www.hookandtackle.com

Rockport Shoes
220 Donald Lynch Blvd.
Marlboro MA 01752

800-762-5767
www.rockport.com

Shoes For Crews
1400 Centrepark Blvd.,
    Suite 310
West Palm Beach FL 33401-7403
800-523-4448; 561-683-5090
www.shoesforcrews.com

Sperry Top-Sider (product of
    Stride Rite Co.)
191 Spring St.
Lexington MA 01421
617-824-6000
www.striderite.com

BOAT SHOWS

The National Marine Manu-
facturers Association organizes
the largest and most popular boat
shows across the country. For more
information on local shows,
contact

NMMA
200 E. Randolph Dr., Suite 5100
Chicago IL 60601
312-946-6200
www.nmma.org

SCHOOLS AND ASSOCIATIONS
FOR WOMEN BOATERS

Becoming an Outdoors-Woman
Dr. Christine Thomas
University of Wisconsin–
    Stevens Point
College of Natural Resouces
Stevens Point WI 54481
715-346-4185
bowwomen@snip.net
www.state.nj.us/dep/fgw/bowhome.
    htm

Ladies, Let's Go Fishing
P.O. Box 550429
Fort Lauderdale FL 33355
954-475-9068
billfishbetty@hotmail.com
www.ladiesletsgofishing.com

Sea Sense—Women's Sailing
  and Powerboating School
P.O. Box 1961
Saint Petersburg, FL 33731
800-332-1404; 727-332-1404
info@seasenseboating.com
www.seasenseboating.com

Women Anglers of Minnesota
P.O. Box 580653
Minneapolis MN 55458-0653
612-339-1322
fishincj@aol.com
www.geocities.com/Heartland/
  7997/wam.htm

Women of Watersports
5220 E. Colonial Dr.
Orlando FL 32807
407-380-0734
www.wowsports.org

Women's Flyfishing
P.O. Box 243-963
Anchorage AK 99524
907-274-7113
ckleinkauf@micronet.net
www.halcyon.com/wffn/index.htm

Women's Scuba Association
6966 S. Atlantic Ave.
New Smyrna Beach FL 32169
904-426-5757
www.womenscuba.org

SEAMANSHIP AND BOATING SAFETY CLASSES

Most listings are for mixed classes
for men and women.

Boating Safety Institute of
  America
800-237-1708
boatsafe@aol.com
www.boatsafety.org

BoatU.S.
www.boatus.com/courseline

Boatwise
72 Woodman Rd.
So. Hampton NH 03827
800-698-7373
boatwise@tiac.net
www.boatwiseclasses.com

Chapman School of Seamanship
4343 S.E. Saint Lucie Blvd.
Stuart FL 34997
800-225-2841; 561-283-8130
info@chapman.org
www.chapman.org

National Association of State
  Boating Law Administrators
  (NASBLA)
P.O. Box 11099
Lexington KY 40512-1099
606-225-9487
nasbla@aol.com
www.nasbla.org

National Safe Boating Council,
  Inc. (NSBC)
P.O. Box 1058
Delaware OH 43015-1058
740-666-3009
nsbcdirect@safeboatingcouncil.org
www.safeboatingcouncil.org

Nautical Know How, Inc.
5102 S.E. Nassau Terrace
Stuart FL 34997
888-297-2076
www.boatsafe.com

U.S. Coast Guard Auxiliary
www.uscgaux.org/cgauxweb/public/
  tbclass.htm

U.S. Coast Guard Office of
  Boating Safety
Infoline@navcen.uscg.mil
www.uscgboating.org

United States Power Squadrons
P.O. Box 30423
Raleigh NC 27622
888-FOR-USPS (888-367-8777)
www.usps.org

BOAT CLUBS

Rentals and shared ownership

Anna Maria Boat Club
5323 Marina Dr.
Holmes Beach FL 34217
941-778-7990
www.home.earthlink.net/
  ~boatclub/

Club Nautico Headquarters
3149 J. P. Curci Dr., #1A-1
Pembroke Park FL 33009-3834
800-BoatRen (800-262-8736);
  800-NAUTICO
  (800-628-8426)
www.boatrent.com

Seaforth Boating Club
1641 Quivira Way
San Diego CA 92109
888-834-BOAT (888-834-2628)

Index